Congress and the Bible
A Historical Perspective

James C. Kahler

Gracious Christian Living, Inc.
1911 SW Campus Drive, #684, Federal Way, WA 98023

Copyright © 2013 James C. Kahler

All rights reserved. With the exception of brief quotations for the purpose of review or comment, no part of this book may be reproduced, stored in a retrieval system, or transmitted in any form or by any means —electronic, photocopy, recorded, or otherwise, without prior permission of publisher, Gracious Christian Living, Inc., 1911 SW Campus Drive, #684, Federal Way, WA 98023.

ISBN 978-0-615-37685-1

Printed in the United States of America

For additional information about historical facsimiles, resources for Christian leaders, and teaching aids, please visit us online at
www.kingjamesbiblestore.com

Table of Contents

CHAPTER ONE
The Bible and the Planting of Jamestown and Massachusetts Bay 1

CHAPTER TWO
The Bible and the Early Documents of the Thirteen Colonies 9

CHAPTER THREE
The Bible and the Continental Congress 25

CHAPTER FOUR
The Bible and the Founding Fathers 45

CHAPTER FIVE
Robert Aitken's Bible 73

CHAPTER SIX
The Bible and the U.S. Congress 91

EPILOGUE
What Role Should the Bible Have in America Today? 101

INDEX OF PICTURES AND IMAGES 109

NOTES 112

Dedication

This book has been produced by Gracious Christian Living, as part of a limited—edition presentation set given to the members of the United States Congress in March 2013.

It is dedicated to the men and women, past and present, who have served and sacrificed as members of the United States Congress. May we as American citizens never forget the burdens and responsibilities they bear, and our duty to uphold them in prayer.

> I exhort therefore, that, first of all, supplications, prayers, intercessions, and giving of thanks, be made for all men;
>
> For kings, and for all that are in authority; that we may lead a quiet and peaceable life in all godliness and honesty.
>
> I Timothy 2:1—2

Preface

Congress and the *Bible*—these are two words you seldom see paired in the same sentence, this in spite of a long-running history in which the two have been intertwined. To pinpoint an exact time when this relationship commenced would be difficult indeed. However, the fact that such a relationship existed from the earliest days of our Union is impossible to deny, especially when one considers Continental Congress endorsement of the Bible printed by Robert Aitken in 1782.[i]

Throughout American history our legislators have recognized the Bible's value. For example, the Bible was cited by our Founding Fathers more than any other source during the 1770s.[ii] Numbers of our legislators have quoted the Scripture and promoted its circulation, considering it relevant to contemporary society. And for these reasons, Scripture is found on public and government buildings across the nation, carved on memorial blocks of the Washington Monument, painted upon the walls of the Library of Congress, and the list goes on and on.

> *"It is impossible to rightly govern the world without God and the Bible."*
>
> George Washington

To properly explore the relationship between Congress and the Bible, the first two chapters of this book consider the historical events and documents that preceded or paralleled the formation of the Continental Congress. To simply begin on September 5, 1774, when the First Continental Congress convened in Carpenters' Hall in Philadelphia, omits necessary background material required to reveal the Bible's influence upon Congress. Even before there was a Congress, the Bible and religion were already exercising an influence upon colonial America and those who would eventually participate in Congress.

Edward Savage's engraving, based on Robert Edge Pine's painting of the presentation of the Declaration of Independence to the Continental Congress, is considered one of the most realistic renditions of this historic event. Jefferson is the tall person depositing the Declaration of Independence on the table. Benjamin Franklin sits to his right. John Hancock sits behind the table. Fellow committee members John Adams, Roger Sherman, and Robert R. Livingston stand (left to right) behind Jefferson—**Library of Congress.**

The Signers of the Declaration of Independence
by Edward Savage after a painting by Robert Edge Pine, ca. 1776.

The third chapter proceeds by noticing the Bible's relationship to the Continental Congress. Much time is spent here, since the thrust of the book is to demonstrate that the Bible and Congress were connected from the latter's inception. Next we turn to the Founders and the Bible. Then, chapter five deals with the Aitken Bible while chapter six lists a number of instances in which the U.S. Congress has involved itself with the Bible.

In the end, you will be brought face to face with the undeniable fact of the matter: the Bible has influenced Congress. To what degree, we will allow historians and theologians to debate; however, what needs no debate is the existence of the relationship between Congress and the Bible.

CHAPTER ONE

THE BIBLE AND THE PLANTING OF JAMESTOWN AND MASSACHUSETTS BAY

Two Important Settlements

In the seventeenth century, British emigrants sailed to the eastern seaboard of North America. Many did so for religious reasons, so that they could worship God in ways deemed unacceptable in Europe.[iii] Of the places inhabited by these early settlers, two of the earliest and most prominent were Jamestown and Massachusetts Bay. The activities that took place in these locations give us a glimpse of the relevance of Scripture during the planting of these settlements.

Jamestown

The Great Citie
by Keith Rocco.
Public Domain.

Jamestown began with a charter issued in 1606 by King James I of England to the Virginia Company of London, a group of investors. Even though this was largely a business venture, it did not take long for the Bible to be woven into the enterprise.

By the 1660s, more than 50 years after the first settlers landed on the island, Jamestown had reached its zenith. Its residents were a mixture of merchants, officials, innkeepers, indentured servants, and slaves.

Congress and the Bible - A Historical Perspective

King James issued "Instructions for the Government of Virginia," which directed that governing councils be formed. One of the obligations of these councils was to assure that the "true word and service of God, according to the rites and services of the Church of England, be preached, planted, and used in the colonies and among the neighboring savages."[iv] The king, who had only two years before commissioned a revision of the Bishop's Bible, was now interested in the Bible being a vital part of the daily life in Virginia. While the Bible was incumbent to the Virginia Company of London's mission, gold, silver, and copper were more important. This is demonstrated by a reading of the first charter of Virginia, which reveals that of 3,805 words, only 98 deal with God.[v]

In December 1606 three ships—the Discovery, the Godspeed, and the Susan Constant—set sail for Virginia. Under the direction of Captain Christopher Newport, 144 mostly homeless, single men left London, intent on finding wealth in the New World; it would not be until 1621 that Jamestown would have any female residents.

The Landing of John Smith
Postcards, Prints and Photographs, ca.1906. Library of Virginia.
Public Domain.

On board the Susan Constant was a man who stood in contrast to most of the other men. Robert Hunt (1568–1608) was an Anglican priest who was regarded by his peers as being saintly, honest, and courageous. After the ships arrived in Jamestown in 1607, Hunt arduously preached twice every Sunday, led prayers twice a day, and administered the Lord's Supper once every three months.[vi]

To facilitate worship, he set up church in a couple primitive settings—first under an old ship's sail, and then in a barn-like structure.

After Hunt's death in 1608, one of his successors, Alexander Whitaker (1585–1617), initiated a ministry to the Indians, a ministry that had been written into the colony's charter by James I.

The Baptism of Pocahontas
by John Gadsby Chapman, ca. 1840.
Public Domain.

In stark contrast to their dreams, the Jamestown settlers did not find the abundance of gold, silver, and copper for which they were seeking. Instead, they experienced disappointment and death by sickness and marauding Indians. This led some disillusioned young men to return to London, where they reported a grim tale of ruin and devastation. Consequently, Sir Thomas Gates was dispatched to Jamestown to bring order out of chaos, order effected through martial law. The "Laws Divine, Moral, and Martial" enforced religion through the sword; yet, despite the presence of enforced religion, by the early 1620s Indians were being driven from their lands and massacred. Hence, while the Bible had small presence in the formative period at Jamestown, it was often subordinate to wealth, enforced by the sword, and disobeyed.

Massachusetts Bay

Massachusetts Bay was settled under different circumstances than those of Jamestown; it was settled, in part, by English Calvinists known as Puritans. These Puritans were part of the Church of England who believed that the Protestant Reformation was not progressing there as it should. To them, the Church of England had retained unbiblical practices such as the priesthood, observance of holy days, elaborate church decorations, and kneeling during the service.[vii] Furthermore, while the Puritans wanted the Church of England to be "purified," some in their number believed that this would never happen. The only answer was to separate from the church. These particular Puritans, who were a small minority, eventually became known as Separatists.

King James I of England and VI of Scotland (1566–1625)
by Sir Anthony Van Dyck.
Public Domain.

England, under the kingship of James I (ruled 1603–1625), did not allow much room for dissenting Puritanism. This was clearly demonstrated by the Hampton Court Conference (January 14, 16, & 18, 1604),[viii] an ecclesiastical conference called by James to settle the differences between the Church of England and the Puritans. After three days of sessions, the conference ended with two memorable outcomes: first, the principle grievances of the Puritans were mostly disregarded; in fact, a royal proclamation gave Puritan ministers until November 30 of that year to conform. Second, a recommendation of Puritan scholar Dr. John Reynolds (or Rainolds) to undertake a new translation of the Bible was accepted. This translation would later bear the king's name—the King James Bible.

One group of Separatists resolved to flee to Holland so they could worship God according to the dictates of their own consciences. However, their well-laid plans did not unfold as they had hoped, for the sailors they had hired to take them to Holland betrayed them to the English officials, who, in turn, captured and imprisoned the men of the party. These men were undaunted and, upon release from prison, were ready to try again to reach Holland. This time they were successful, and in 1609 three hundred men, women, and children arrived safely in the city of Leyden (or Leiden). While Holland afforded the Separatists more religious freedom, it also brought hardship. The Dutch placed work restrictions upon the Separatists, which forced their families to labor long hours. Because the boys and girls were working, they could not attend school. In addition, the religious climate in Holland, while freer that that of England, nevertheless exercised undesirable influences upon the Separatist children.[ix] The time had come for another move.

The Separatists soon set their sights on the New World, and possessed "a great hope and inward zeall . . . of laying some good foundation, or at least to make some way therunto, for the propagating and advancing the gospel of the kingdom of Christ in those remote parts of the world; yea, though they should be but even as stepping-stones unto others for the performing of so great a work."[x] Through the assistance of Sir Edwin Sandys, the Separatists secured permission in 1620 from the Virginia Company of London to settle in the northern part of Virginia, a colony with an expansive coastline. Although King James refused to grant the Separatists an official guarantee of religious toleration, he assured them that they would not be persecuted if they lived in peace.

Because a voyage across the Atlantic would be costly, the Separatists sought financiers for their venture. They found such backers in a group of London businessmen known as the Adventurers. The arrangements were straightforward: the Adventurers would underwrite the trip to Virginia, and the Separatists would send the Adventurers a portion of their profits from the first seven years.

Not all of the English Separatists residing in Holland prepared to sail to Virginia: only approximately one tenth chose to make the trip. Originally, two ships were to sail from England to Virginia: the *Mayflower* and the *Speedwell*. However, the latter proved unseaworthy and was not able to make the voyage. Of the *Speedwell's* passengers, 20 returned to London, at least two returned to Leyden, and 11 boarded the *Mayflower*. Most people today, following the lead of William Bradford,[xi] refer to the passengers of the *Mayflower* as the *Pilgrims*. On September 16, 1620, the *Mayflower* set sail from Plymouth, England, with 102 passengers. During the course of the 66-day voyage, baby Oceanus Hopkins was born. Also,

Pilgrim Fathers boarding the Mayflower
by Bernard Gribble ca.1926.
Public Domain.

William Brutten, a servant who was but a youth, died. Due to a terrible storm and navigational errors, the *Mayflower* failed to stick to her charted course; thus, on November 21, instead of reaching the coast of Virginia, the Pilgrims' vessel reached present-day Provincetown, Massachusetts. Here the passengers remained aboard the *Mayflower* for a month while a search party explored for a suitable site for a new colony. It was during this time that Peregrine White was delivered, the first European child born in New England; it was also during this time that the Mayflower Compact was drafted and signed. Forty-one men signed this document, including Puritans, hired men, and servants.

The Mayflower Compact, according to historian Paul Johnson, was "based upon the original Biblical covenant between God and the Israelites."[xii] It established republican government, whereby law and order could be maintained within the colony. Men were viewed as equals who were responsible for the "general good" of society. And while it would prove immediately beneficial to the Pilgrims, it also would prove distantly beneficial to the United States of America. The seeds planted in the Mayflower Compact would be scattered by the winds of time and would find themselves implanted in the Declaration of Independence and the U.S. Constitution.

MAYFLOWER COMPACT

In the name of God Amen. We whose names are underwritten, the loyall subjects of our dread sovereign Lord King James by the grace of God, of great Britaine, Franc, & Ireland kind, defender of the faith, &c.

Having undertaken for the Glory of God, and Advancement of the Christian Faith, and the Honour of our King and Country, a voyage to plant the first colony in the northern Parts of Virginia; do by these Presents, solemnly and mutually in the Presence of God and of one another, covenant and combine ourselves together into a civil Body Politick, for our better Ordering and Preservation, and Furtherance of the Ends aforesaid; And by Virtue hereof to enact, constitute, and frame, such just and equal Laws, Ordinances, Acts, Constitutions and Offices, from time to time, as shall be thought most meet and convenient for the General good of the Colony; unto which we promise all due Submission and Obedience.

In witness whereof we have hereunder subscribed our names at Cap-Codd the 11 of November, in the year of the raigne of our sovereign Lord King James of England, France, & Ireland the eighteenth and of Scotland the fiftie fourth. An: Com. 1620.[xiii]

The Signing of the Mayflower Compact
by T. H. Matheson, engraving by Gauthier, ca. 1859.
Public Domain.

On December 21 the Pilgrims disembarked from the Mayflower, ready to begin their life in the New World. Although they would face a difficult winter, witness the death of many of their fellows, and later struggle with toleration of others' beliefs that did not match their own, they would press on. And so would the influence of the Bible. In fact, because the Puritans taught their children to read the Bible, Massachusetts Bay became one of the most literate places in the world.[xiv]

Summary

Not all the early settlements in British North America possessed a biblical foundation, yet myriads did. Also, not all the early emigrants came to the New World for religious freedom, yet multitudes did. And those who came for religious reasons often brought with them the Scriptures. Therefore, from the beginning, the Bible had a presence in settlements. Naturally, the Bible and religion also had a presence in the colonies, including the colonies' early founding documents. This leads us to our next chapter.

CHAPTER TWO

THE BIBLE AND THE EARLY DOCUMENTS OF THE THIRTEEN ORIGINAL COLONIES

Beginnings

History is a collection of cause and effect relationships. This means that behind most actions are reasons that lead to results. We see this in the inception of our nation's earliest colonies. Quite simply, many early British emigrants came to North America (the effect) so that they could worship God in ways deemed unacceptable in Europe (the cause). And while religious freedom was not the only cause that drove these individuals to settle in America, it was often one of the primary causes. Further, if religion was often a cause for the planting of colonies—and it was, then the early documents should somewhere reflect this—and they do. Therefore it is pertinent that we notice some of what these documents have to say about the Bible and religion.

Before we proceed, one word needs to be said about the selected references. They have been culled from legal and political—not religious—documents. The charters and constitutions were not specifically written to articulate theological beliefs. In addition, the religious sections of these documents are relatively small. First and foremost, these charters and constitutions were written as business contracts and legal devices; however, they were often written by individuals who possessed religious backgrounds and desires. Also, they were generally directed to people of faith; therefore, it is quite understandable that they would contain religious terminology and phraseology.

Virginia

Virginia's charter of 1606, issued by James I of England, contained the following sentence:

> We, greatly commending, and graciously accepting of, their Desires for the Furtherance of so noble a Work, which may, by the Providence of Almighty God, hereafter tend to the Glory of his Divine Majesty, in propagating of Christian Religion to such People, as yet live in Darkness and miserable Ignorance of the true Knowledge and Worship of God, and may in time bring the Infidels and Savages, living in those parts, to human Civility, and to a settled and quiet Government: DO, by these our Letters Patents, graciously accept of, and agree to, their humble and well-intended Desires . . .[xv]

Religion was present in Virginia's Declaration of Rights, adopted unanimously on June 12, 1776. The Declaration of Rights would later, in 1830, be incorporated into Virginia's constitution as Article 1, Section 16. It affirmed:

> That religion, or the duty which we owe to our Creator, and the manner of discharging it, can be directed only by reason and conviction, not by force or violence; and therefore all men are equally entitled to the free exercise of religion, according to the dictates of conscience; and that it is the mutual duty of all to practice Christian forbearance, love, and charity towards each other.[xvi]

Source: Edward S. Ellis, *Elliss' History of the United States* (Minneapolis: Wester Book Syndicate, 1899), I:312.

Massachusetts

In 1629, Charles I of Great Britain issued Massachusetts Bay a charter that declared:

> . . . our said People, Inhabitants there, may be soe religiously, peaceablie, and civilly governed, as their good Life and orderlie Conversacon, male wynn and incite the Natives of Country, to the Knowledg and Obedience of the onlie true God and Saulor of Mankinde, and the Christian Fayth, which in our Royall Intencon, and the Adventurers free Profession, is the principall Ende of this Plantacion.[xvii]

King Charles I
by Anthony van Dyck, ca. 1645.
Public Domain.

Notice the "principal end" of the plantation (or colony): the conversion of the natives to Christianity. This should not seem unusual, for this was also an objective found in Virginia's charter of 1606, Maryland's charter of 1632, Connecticut's charter of 1662, Carolina's charter of 1663, Rhode Island's charter of 1663, and Pennsylvania's charter of 1681.

Article 2 of Part 1 (A Declaration of Rights) of Massachusetts's constitution of 1780 reveals the importance of religion to Massachusetts during this time.

> It is the right as well as the duty of all men in society, publicly and at stated seasons, to worship the Supreme Being, the great Creator and Preserver of the universe. And no subject shall be hurt, molested, or restrained, in his person, liberty, or estate, for worshipping God in the manner and season most agreeable to the dictates of his own conscience, or for his religious profession or sentiments, provided he doth not disturb the public peace or obstruct others in their religious worship.[xviii]

New Hampshire

Part 1 (The Bill of Rights) of New Hampshire's constitution of 1784 contained two articles dealing with religion.

Article 5
Every individual has a natural and unalienable right to worship GOD according to the dictates of his own conscience, and reason; and no subject shall be hurt, molested, or restrained in his person, liberty or estate for worshipping GOD, in the manner and season most agreeable to the dictates of his own conscience, or for his religious profession, sentiments or persuasion; provided he doth not disturb the public peace, or disturb others, in their religious worship.[xix]

Article 6
As morality and piety, rightly grounded on evangelical principles, will give the best and greatest security to government, and will lay in the hearts of men the strongest obligations to due subjection; and as the knowledge of these, is most likely to be propagated through a society by the institution of the public worship of the DEITY, and of public instruction in morality and religion; therefore, to promote those important purposes, the people of this state have a right to impower, and do hereby fully impower the legislature to authorize from time to time, the several towns, parishes, bodies corporate, or religious societies within this state, to make adequate provision at their own expence, for the support and maintenance of public protestant teachers of piety, religion and morality . . .[xx]

Source: Edward Taylor, *The Model History*
(Chicago, IL: Scott, Foresman and Company, 1900)

Maryland

In 1632, Charles I issued Maryland a charter that specified:

> Whereas our well beloved and right trusty Subject Caecilius Calvert, Baron of Baltimore, in our Kingdom of Ireland, Son and Heir of George Calvert, Knight, late Baron of Baltimore, in our said Kingdom of Ireland, treading in the steps of his Father, being animated with a laudable, and pious Zeal for extending the Christian Religion, and also the Territories of our Empire, hath humbly besought Leave of us, that he may transport, by his own Industry, and Expense, a numerous Colony of the English Nation, to a certain Region, herein after described, in a Country hitherto uncultivated, in the Parts of America, and partly occupied by Savages, having no knowledge of the Divine Being, and that all that Region, with some certain Privileges, and Jurisdiction, appertaining unto the wholesome Government, and State of his Colony and Region aforesaid, may by our Royal Highness be given, granted and confirmed unto him, and his Heirs.[xxi]

Article 33 of "A Declaration of Rights" of Maryland's constitution of 1776 pronounced:

> That, as it is the duty of every man to worship God in such manner as he thinks most acceptable to him; all persons, professing the Christian religion, are equally entitled to protection in their religious liberty; wherefore no person ought by any law to be molested in his person or estate on account of his religious persuasion or profession, or for his religious practice; unless, under colour of religion, any man shall disturb the good order, peace or safety of the State, or shall infringe the laws of morality, or injure others, in their natural, civil, or religious rights; nor ought any person to be compelled to frequent or maintain, or contribute, unless on contract, to maintain any particular place of worship, or any particular ministry; yet the Legislature may, in their discretion, lay a general and equal tax for the support of the Christian religion. . . .[xxii]

Source: Edward Taylor, *The Model History*
(Chicago, IL: Scott, Foresman and Company, 1900).

Connecticut

Connecticut's charter of 1662, issued by Charles II, asserted:

> . . . Imprisonment or other Punishment upon Offenders and Delinquents according to the Curse of other Corporations within this our Kingdom of England, and the same Laws, Fines, Mulcts and Executions, to alter, change, revoke, annul, release, or pardon under their Common Seal, as by the said General Assembly, or the major Part of them shall be thought fit, and for the directing, ruling and disposing of all other Matters and things, whereby Our said People Inhabitants there, may be so religiously, peaceably and civilly governed, as their good Life and orderly Conversation may win and invite the Natives of the Country to the Knowledge and Obedience of the only true GOD, and He Saviour of Mankind, and the Christian Faith, which in Our Royal Intentions, and the adventurers free Possession, is the only and principal End of this Plantation . . .[xxiii]

King Charles II
by John Michael Wright, ca. 1661.
Public Domain.

Rhode Island

On March 7, 1638 a group of men banished from Massachusetts signed the Portsmouth Compact, establishing the settlement of Portsmouth, which is now a town in Rhode Island. It is believed to be the first document to sever political and religious ties with Great Britain. The Portsmouth Compact, also known as the Coddington Compact, stated:

> We, whose names are underwritten, do here solemnly in the presence of Jehovah incorporate ourselves into a bodie politick and as He shall help, will submit our persons, lives and estates, unto our Lord Jesus Christ, the King of Kings, and Lord of Lords, and to all those perfect and most absolute laws of His given us in His Holy Word of truth, to be guided and judged thereby.[xxiv]

Charles II issued a charter to Rhode Island and Providence Plantations in 1663, in which the following was cited concerning Rhode Island's early settlers:

> . . . they, pursueing, with peaceable and loyall minces, their sober, serious and religious intentions, of goalie edifieing themselves, and one another, in the holie Christian ffaith and worshipp as they were perswaded; together with the gaineing over and conversione of the poore ignorant Indian natives, in those partes of America, to the sincere professione and obedienc of the same faith and worship, did, not onlie by the consent and good encouragement of our royall progenitors, transport themselves out of this kingdome of England into America . . .[xxv]

Source: Israel Smith Clare, *Illustrated Universal History* (Philadelphia: J. C. McCurdy & Co., 1878), 456.

Delaware

William Penn issued Delaware a charter in 1701, which articulated:

> BECAUSE no People can be truly happy, though under the greatest Enjoyment of Civil Liberties, if abridged of the Freedom of their Consciences, as to their Religious Profession and Worship: And Almighty God being the only Lord of Conscience, Father of Lights and Spirits; and the Author as well as Object of all divine Knowledge, Faith and Worship, who only doth enlighten the Minds, and persuade and convince the Understandings of People, I do hereby grant and declare, That no Person or Persons, inhabiting In this Province or Territories, who shall confess and acknowledge One almighty God, the Creator, Upholder and Ruler of the World; and professes him or themselves obliged to live quietly under the Civil Government, shall be in any Case molested or prejudiced, in his or their Person or Estate, because of his or their conscientious Persuasion or Practice, nor be compelled to frequent or maintain any religious Worship, Place or Ministry, contrary to his or their Mind, or to do or suffer any other Act or Thing, contrary to their religious Persuasion.[xxvi]

Article 22 of Delaware's constitution of 1776 required officeholders to profess belief in the Trinity and the divine inspiration of the Bible.

> I, A B. do profess faith in God the Father, and in Jesus Christ His only Son, and in the Holy Ghost, one God, blessed for evermore; and I do acknowledge the holy scriptures of the Old and New Testament to be given by divine inspiration.[xxvii]

Source: Edward S. Ellis, *Ellis's History of the United States* (Minneapolis: Wester Book Syndicate, 1899), IV:1255.

North Carolina

Carolina's charter of 1663, issued by Charles II, mentioned:

> Whereas our right trusty, and right well beloved cousins and counsellors, Edward Earl of Clarendon, our high chancellor of England, and George Duke of Albemarle, master of our horse and captain general of all our forces, our right trusty and well beloved William Lord Craven, John Lord Berkley, our right trusty and well beloved counsellor, Anthony Lord Ashley, chancellor of our exchequer, Sir George Carteret, knight and baronet, vice chamberlain of our household, and our trusty and well beloved Sir William Berkley, knight, and Sir John Colleton, knight and baronet, being excited with a laudable and pious zeal for the propagation of the Christian faith, and the enlargement of our empire and dominions, have humbly besought leave of us, by their industry and charge, to transport and make an ample colony of our subjects, natives of our kingdom of England, and elsewhere within our dominions, unto a certain country hereafter described, in the parts of America not yet cultivated or planted, and only inhabited by some barbarous people, who have no knowledge of Almighty God.[xxviii]

Article 32 of "The Constitution or Form of Government" of North Carolina's constitution of 1776 required officeholders to believe in God and the divine authority of the Bible.

> That no person, who shall deny the being of God or the truth of the Protestant religion, or the divine authority either of the Old or New Testaments, or who shall hold religious principles incompatible with the freedom and safety of the State, shall be capable of holding any office or place of trust or profit in the civil department within this State.[xxix]

South Carolina

Article 38 of South Carolina's constitution of 1778 contained a lengthy statement concerning religion.

> That all persons and religious societies who acknowledge that there is one God, and a future state of rewards and punishments, and that God is publicly to be worshipped, shall be freely tolerated. The Christian Protestant religion shall be deemed, and is hereby constituted and declared to be, the established religion of this State. That all denominations of Christian Protestants in this State, demeaning themselves peaceably and faithfully, shall enjoy equal religious and civil privileges. To accomplish this desirable purpose without injury to the religious property of those societies of Christians which are by law already incorporated for the purpose of religious worship, and to put it fully into the power of every other society of Christian Protestants, either already formed or hereafter to be formed, to obtain the like incorporation, it is hereby constituted, appointed, and declared that the respective societies of the Church of England that are already formed in this State for the purpose of religious worship shall still continue incorporate and hold the religious property now in their possession. And that whenever fifteen or more male persons, not under twenty-one years of age, professing the Christian Protestant religion, and agreeing to unite themselves In a society for the purposes of religious worship, they shall, (on complying with the terms hereinafter mentioned) be, and be constituted a church, and be esteemed and regarded in law as of the established religion of the State, and on a petition to the legislature shall be entitled to be incorporated and to enjoy equal privileges. That every society of Christians so formed

Source: Benson J. Lossing, *An Outline History of the United States* (New York: Sheldon & Company, 1878), 119.

shall give themselves a name or denomination by which they shall be called and known in law, and all that associate with them for the purposes of worship shall be esteemed as belonging to the society so called. But that previous to the establishment and incorporation of the respective societies of every denomination as aforesaid, and in order to entitle them thereto, each society so petitioning shall have agreed to and subscribed in a book the following five articles, without which no agreement firm union of men upon presence of religion shall entitle them to be incorporated and esteemed as a church of the established religion of this State: as belonging to the society so called.

1st. That there is one eternal God, and a future state of rewards and punishments.

2d. That God is publicly to be worshiped.

3d. That the Christian religion is the true religion

4th. That the holy scriptures of the Old and New Testaments are of divine inspiration, and are the rule of faith and practice.

5th. That it is lawful and the duty of every man being thereunto called by those that govern, to bear witness to the truth. . . .[xxx]

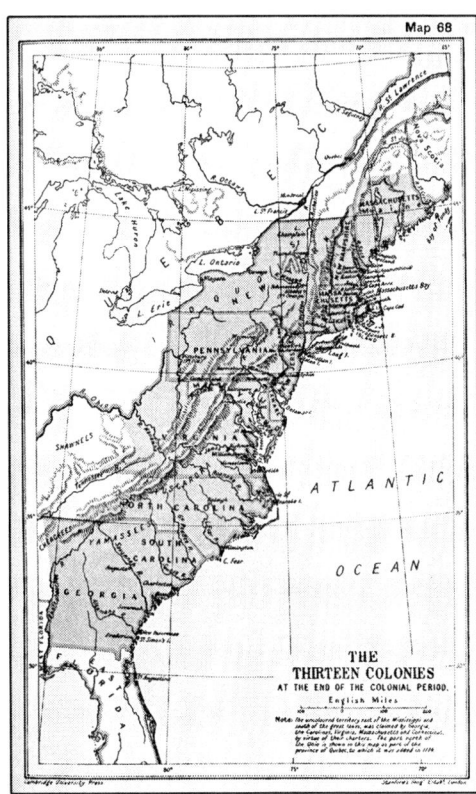

The Thirteen Colonies at the End of the Colonial Period
Cambridge Modern History Atlas, 1912.

New Jersey

Chapter 16 of "The Charter of Fundamental Laws of West New Jersey, Agreed Upon" (1676) proclaimed:

> That no men, nor number of men upon earth, hath power or authority to rule over men's consciences in religious matters, therefore it is consented, agreed and ordained, that no person or persons whatsoever within the said Province, at any time or times hereafter, shall be any ways upon any presence whatsoever, called in question, or in the least punished or hurt, either in person, estate, or priviledge, for the sake of his opinion, judgment, faith or worship towards God in matters of religion. But that all and every such person, and persons may from time to time, and at all times, freely and fully have, and enjoy his and their judgments, and the exercises of their consciences in matters of religious worship throughout all the said Province.[xxxi]

Article 19 of New Jersey's constitution of 1776 stipulated:

> That there shall be no establishment of any one religious sect in this Province, in preference to another; and that no Protestant inhabitant of this Colony shall be denied the enjoyment of any civil right, merely on account of his religious principles; but that all persons, professing a belief in the faith of any Protestant sect who shall demean themselves peaceably under the government, as hereby established, shall be capable of being elected into any office of profit or trust, or being a member of either branch of the Legislature, and shall fully and freely enjoy every privilege and immunity, enjoyed by others their fellow subjects.[xxxii]

Colonial Seals of
East and West Jersey

Source: Arthur C. Perry,
American History
(New York, NY: American Book Company, 1913)

New York

Article 38 of New York's constitution of 1777 expressed freedom of religion.

> And whereas we are required, by the benevolent principles of rational liberty, not only to expel civil tyranny, but also to guard against that spiritual oppression and intolerance wherewith the bigotry and ambition of weak and wicked priests and princes have scourged mankind, this convention doth further, in the name and by the authority of the good people of this State, ordain, determine, and declare, that the free exercise and enjoyment of religious profession and worship, without discrimination or preference, shall forever hereafter be allowed, within this State, to all mankind: Provided, That the liberty of conscience, hereby granted, shall not be so construed as to excuse acts of licentiousness, or justify practices inconsistent with the peace or safety of this State.[xxxiii]

Pennsylvania

The charter that Charles II issued to William Penn in 1681 included the following sentence:

> CHARLES the Second, by the Grace of God, King of England, Scotland, France, and Ireland, Defender of the Faith, &c. To all whom these presents shall come, Greets. WHEREAS Our Trustie and wellbeloved Subject WILLIAM PENN, Esquire, Sonne and heire of Sir WILLIAM PENN deceased, out of a commendable Desire to enlarge our English Empire, and promote such usefull comodities as may bee of Benefit to us and Our Dominions, as also to reduce the savage Natives by gentle and just mamlers to the Love of Civil Societie and Christian Religion, hath humbley besought Leave of Us to transport an ample Colonie unto a certaine Countrey hereinafter described.[xxxiv]

Portrait of William Penn
Artist Unknown.
Source: Wikimedia Commons.
Public Domain.

Article 2 of "A Declaration of the Rights of the Inhabitants of The Commonwealth or State of Pennsylvania" of Pennsylvania's constitution of (1776) asserted:

> That all men have a natural and unalienable right to worship Almighty God according to the dictates of their own consciences and understanding: And that no man ought or of right can be compelled to attend any religious worship, or erect or support anyplace of worship, or maintain any ministry, contrary to, or against, his own free will and consent: Nor can any man, who acknowledges the being of a God, be justly deprived or abridged of any civil right as a citizen, on account of his religious sentiments or peculiar mode of religious worship: And that no authority can or ought to be vested in, or assumed by any power whatever, that shall in any case interfere with, or in any manner controul the right of conscience in the free exercise of religious worship.[xxxv]

Section 10 of a "Plan or Frame of Government for The Commonwealth or State of Pennsylvania" of (1776) required officeholders to affirm:

> I do believe in one God, the creator and governor of the universe, the rewarder of the good and the punisher of the wicked.
>
> And I do acknowledge the Scriptures of the Old and New Testament to be given by Divine inspiration.[xxxvi]

The Birth of Pennsylvania
by Jean Leon Gerome Ferris, ca. 1680.
Public Domain.

Georgia

In 1732 George II of Great Britain issued a charter to Georgia, which maintained:

> Also we do, for ourselves and successors, declare, by these presents, that all and every the persons which shall happen to be born within the said province, and every of their children and posterity, shall have and enjoy all liberties, franchises and immunities of free denizens and natural born subjects, within any of our dominions, to all intents and purposes, as if abiding and born within this our kingdom of Great-Britain, or any other of our dominions And for the greater ease and encouragement of our loving subjects and such others as shall come to inhabit in our said colony, we do by these presents, for us, our heirs and successors, grant, establish and ordain, that forever hereafter, there shall be a liberty of conscience allowed in the worship of God, to all persons inhabiting, or which shall inhabit or be resident within our said provinces and that all such persons, except papists, shall have a free exercise of their religion, so they be contented with the quiet and peaceable enjoyment of the same, not giving offence or scandal to the government.[xxxvii]

Article 61 of Georgia's constitution of 1777 declared:

> All persons whatever shall have the free exercise of their religion; provided it be not repugnant to the peace and safety of the State; and shall not, unless by consent, support any teacher or teachers except those of their own profession.[xxxviii]

Source: Edward S. Ellis, Ellis's History of the United States (Minneapolis: Wester Book Syndicate, 1899), I:280

Summary

What we have seen, through the excerpted parts of these early colonial documents, is that each of the original 13 colonies recognized the importance of the free exercise of religion. Further, a number of these colonies (later called states) identified religion based upon the Bible—Christianity—to be integral to their foundation and furtherance. In light of this evidence, some make the case that the states were founded upon the Bible and Christianity. Others decry such a position, contending that the states' origins were completely secular in nature.

So were the states founded upon the Bible? After all, the evidence demonstrates that religion, particularly Christianity, was often present in their founding documents. The short answer is "somewhat" for the following reason: not all that was contained in (or missing from) these documents was biblical. This does not lead us, however, to deny the importance of the Bible in the founding of states and to espouse a secular position. Instead, it causes us to carefully articulate the role the Bible served in the formation of these documents. A correct and trenchant analysis is this: a majority of the states imbued biblical principles in their founding instruments. For example, to some degree they built upon biblical principles of human dignity, morality, and justice. Yet, they also—for reasons outside the scope of this work—did not prohibit the inhumane capture, transportation, treatment, and selling of slaves from Africa (chattel slavery).[xxxix]

What is critical to understand at this juncture is that most of the states' constitutions did indeed imbue biblical principles. This is because many of the legislators who crafted these constitutions personally, professionally, and politically recognized the value of the Bible, especially in its promotion of morals. Moreover, a number of these legislators also served in the Continental Congress and would help shape that body's view of the Bible.[xl]

CHAPTER THREE

THE BIBLE AND THE CONTINENTAL CONGRESS

Seeds of Unrest

The thirteen original colonies functioned quite independently of one another. However, while the colonies shared little in common by the 1760s—when difficulties began to arise with the mother country—they were linked, nevertheless, by the English language; a common tie to Great Britain; a desire for republican government; and the presence of religion in their founding documents, particularly Protestant Christianity. Furthermore, Protestantism was seen as a religion of liberty; individuals were free to read their Bibles for themselves and draw their own theological conclusions.[xli]

The colonies advantageously exercised their freedoms as British subjects, and as long as they were treated as British subjects possessing British rights, all went well. Howbeit, in 1761 Great Britain raised the ire of many colonists by passing the so-called "writs of assistance," general search warrants that allowed authorized officers to enter the house of any person suspected of smuggling. And while some historians breeze over this event as a mere trifle, John Adams referred to it by stating: "Then and there the child independence was born."[xlii]

Source: Edward S. Ellis, Ellis's *History of the United States* (Minneapolis: Wester Book Syndicate, 1899), II:404

In 1765 Great Britain enacted the Stamp Act, a tax levied to raise revenue to provide for the defense of the colonies following the French and Indian War (1754–1763), known in Europe as the Seven Years' War. This act required items such as legal documents, newspapers, pamphlets, and almanacs to carry a tax stamp. The money generated through the sale of these stamps—as well as the funds raised by the Sugar Act (1764)—was directly applied to the expense of maintaining a standing army in the colonies. Although the taxes generated finances for their own defense, colonial leaders began to resist the new taxes, not so much from an economic standpoint, but rather from a philosophical one. "No taxation without representation" became their clarion call.

Portrait of Benjamin Franklin
by Joseph-Siffred Duplessis, ca.1778.
Public Domain.

Franklin represented Pennsylvania in discussions about the Stamp Act.

As British subjects, the colonists believed that they should possess basic British rights, including the right of representation in regards to taxation. Because they were stripped of this basic right, nine of the 13 colonies sent delegates to New York in October 1765 to convene a "Stamp Act Congress." There delegates called for the repeal of the Stamp Act. In addition, colonial businessmen agreed to stop importing British goods until the act was repealed. The British Parliament responded by repealing the Stamp Act on March 4, 1766. Nevertheless, the repeal was accompanied by another act, the Declaratory Act (1766), which affirmed the right of the British government to pass acts legally binding on the colonies in all cases.

Following the Declaratory Act, Britain issued the Townshend Acts (1767), which levied new taxes on luxury items such as wine, fruit, glass, lead, paint, and tea. Then ensued additional acts such as the Tea Act (1773), the Boston Port Act (1774), the Quebec Acts (1774), and the Coercive Acts (1774), popularly referred to as the "Intolerable Acts" by the colonists. The Coercive Acts were a series of laws meant to punish the colony of Massachusetts for destroying a shipment of tea in 1773, the so-called Boston Tea Party. And while the Coercive Acts began as a Massachusetts verses Great Britain issue, it soon became a colonies versus Great Britain issue, for the other colonies rallied to the support of Massachusetts.

The First Continental Congress Convenes

Portrait of Thomas Jefferson by Rembrandt Peale, ca. 1800.
Public Domain.

The Coercive Acts were like a match thrown on dry timber. Among other things, they: closed the Boston Harbor, limited town meetings within Massachusetts, allowed the trials of royal officials indicted in Massachusetts to be moved to another colony or Great Britain, and permitted British troops to be quartered in unoccupied buildings.

In response, other colonies immediately came to the assistance of Massachusetts. For example, Rhode Island and New York proposed a general congress of the colonies to deal with the situation at hand (May 21 & 23, 1774). Virginia, following the suggestion of Thomas Jefferson, adopted a resolution on May 24 to set apart June 1 as:

A day of fasting, humiliation, and prayer; devoutly to implore the divine interposition, for averting and the heavy calamity which threatens destruction to our civil rights, and the evils of civil war; to give us one heart and one mind firmly to oppose, by all just and proper means, every injury to American rights.[xliii]

One by one the colonies came to the support of Massachusetts. This led the Massachusetts House of Representatives to resolve, on June 17, "that a meeting of Committees, from the several Colonies on this Continent is highly expedient and necessary, to consult upon the present state of the Colonies."[xliv] Moreover, the House also recommended that the meeting take place in Philadelphia on September 1. To arrive in Philadelphia, the delegates had to allow plenty of time for travel. For example, the Massachusetts delegation set out from Boston on August 10, almost a month ahead of the appointed day. They arrived in Philadelphia early, the calendar indicating it was August 29, 1774. Shortly thereafter, delegates from other colonies began arriving as well—some by horseback and others by stagecoach, with the South Carolinians finding transportation by wind and water most feasible.[xlv] Generally it was a dirty, dusty, and wearisome journey. One delegate from Virginia, Richard Bland, however, seemed indefatigable. He declared that he would have gone to Jericho had that biblical city been selected as the meeting place.

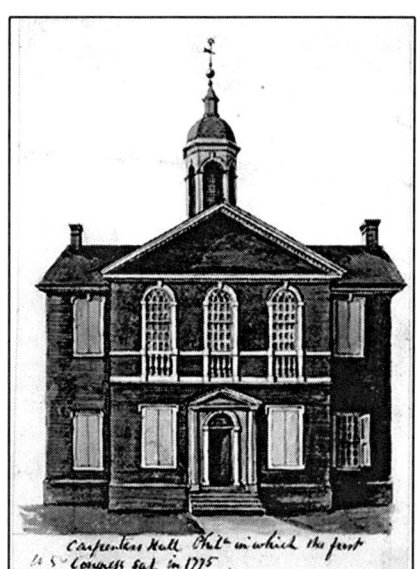

Carpenter's Hall, Philadelphia
by William L. Breton, ca. 1775.
Public Domain.

The delegates convened on September 5 at 10:00 a.m. in the City (or Smith's) Tavern. From there, they walked to Carpenter's Hall,[xlvi] where they voted to remain. It was now time to do business. The matter at hand was to respond to the colonies' grievances with Great Britain, especially their grievances with the Coercive Acts. And while not all the delegates were present the first day, delegates from all thirteen colonies except Georgia would attend the First Continental Congress.[xlvii] Georgia did not send any delegates, probably because it was seeking help from the British to help fight the Indians.

First Prayer in Congress

The First Prayer in Congress
by Tompkins Harrison Matteson, ca. 1848.
Public Domain.

During the proceedings of the second day's session, debate began to wax warm—so warm in fact that it was soon moved by Thomas Cushing to open each day's session with prayer, as to bring harmony to the assembly.[xlviii] Samuel Adams then "asserted that he was no bigot, and could hear a prayer from any gentleman of piety and virtue, who was at the same time a friend to His country."[xlix] He then proceeded to nominate the Rev. Jacob Duché. Recorded in the Journals of Congress is the following entry from September 6, 1774:

> Resolved, That the Rev. Mr. Duché be desired to open the Congress tomorrow morning with prayers, at the Carpenter's Hall, at 9 o'Clock.[l]

The next morning, the Rev. Duché opened Congress by praying and reading Psalm 35. Entered into the Journals of Congress for that day was the following entry:

> Voted, That the thanks of the Congress be given to Mr. Duché, by Mr. Cushing and Mr. Ward, for performing divine Service, and for the excellent prayer, which he composed and deliver'd on the occasion.[li]

The Rev. Duché's prayer and Bible reading so moved delegate John Adams that he wrote about the experience to his wife Abigail, in a letter dated September 16, 1774.

> *Having a Leisure Moment, while the Congress is assembling, I gladly embrace it to write you a Line.*
>
> *When the Congress first met, Mr. Cushing made a Motion, that it should be opened with prayer. It was opposed by Mr. Jay, of New York, and Mr. Rutledge, of South Carolina, because we were so divided in religious sentiments, some Episcopalians, some Quakers, some Aanabaptists, some Presbyterians, and some Congregationalists, that we could not join in the same act of worship. Mr. Samuel Adams arose and said he was no bigot, and could hear a prayer from a gentleman of piety and virtue, who was at the same time a friend to his country. He was a stranger in Philadelphia, but had heard that Mr. Duché (Dushay they pronounce it) deserved that character, and therefore he moved that Mr. Duché, an episcopal clergyman, might be desired to read prayers to the Congress, to-morrow morning. The motion was seconded and passed in the affirmative. Mr. Randolph, our president, waited on Mr. Duché, and received for answer that if his health would permit, he certainly would. Accordingly, next morning he appeared with his clerk and in his pontificals, and read several prayers in the established form; and then read the Collect for the seventh day of September, which was the thirty-fifth Psalm. You must remember this was the next morning after we heard the horrible rumour, of the cannonade of Boston. I never saw a greater effect upon an audience. It seemed as if Heaven had ordained that Psalm to be read on that morning.*

After this Mr. Duché, unexpected to everybody, struck out into an extemporary prayer, which filled the bosom of every man present. I must confess I never heard a better prayer, or one so well pronounced. Episcopalian as he is, Dr. Cooper himself never prayed with such fervor, such ardor, such earnestness and pathos, and in language so elegant and sublime—for America, for the Congress, for The Province of Massachusetts Bay, and especially the town of Boston. It has had an excellent effect upon everybody here. I must beg you to read that Psalm. If there was any faith in the Sortes Biblicae, it would be thought providential.

John Adams
by Asher B. Durand.
Public Domain.

It will amuse your Friends to read this Letter and the thirty-fifth Psalm to them. Read it to your father and Mr. Wibirt. I wonder what our Braintree Churchmen would think of this! Mr. Duché is one of the most ingenious men, and best characters, and greatest orators in the Episcopal order, upon this Continent. Yet a zealous friend of Liberty and his country.

I long to see my dear family. God bless, preserve, and prosper it.

Adieu.[lii]

Thus began a long-standing tradition to open congressional sessions with prayer. Also, the Rev. Jacob Duché continued to minister to the Continental Congress in an unofficial capacity until he was elected Congress's first chaplain on July 9, 1776, a position that continues to this day.

Before the First Continental Congress disbanded, they agreed to send a petition to King George III, addressing their grievances and appealing for the king's help in working out solutions.[liii] Congress also agreed to send an address to the people of Great Britain and an address to those North American colonies that were not represented in Congress (Quebec, St. John's in Nova Scotia, Georgia, and East and West Florida.)

Finally, the delegates resolved on October 22 to convene another congress on May 10, 1775, if their rights were not restored.[liv] On October 26, 1774, the First Continental Congress adjourned. Now it was time to wait for a response from the king.

The Period Between the Continental Congresses

George III refused to respond to Congress's petition, which caused remaining colonial loyalty to the king to further dissipate. This also produced a foreboding sense of impending conflict, a conflict for which the colonists—particularly those from Massachusetts—endeavored to prepare.

On March 23, 1775, orator Patrick Henry—former delegate to the First Continental Congress, and future delegate to the Second Continental Congress—stood before the Virginia House of Burgesses, meeting at St. John's Church in Richmond, and, in a speech for the ages, uttered these enduring words:

> It is in vain, sir, to extentuate the matter. Gentlemen may cry, Peace, Peace—but there is no peace. The war is actually begun! The next gale that sweeps from the north will bring to our ears the clash of resounding arms! Our brethren are already in the field! Why stand we here idle? What is it that gentlemen wish? What would they have? Is life so dear, or peace so sweet, as to be purchased at the price of chains and slavery? Forbid it, Almighty God! I know not what course others may take; but as for me, give me liberty or give me death![lv]

This rousing speech from the fiery patriot helped to spur the independence movement. Characteristically, Henry referenced God and alluded to the Bible. Notice the similarity between Henry's "Gentleman may cry, Peace, Peace—but there is no peace" Jeremiah 6:14–"They have healed also the hurt of the daughter of my people slightly, saying, Peace, peace; when there is no peace." Also notice the resemblance between "Why stand we here idle" to "And about the eleventh hour he went out, and found others standing idle, and saith unto them, Why stand ye here all the day idle" (Matthew 20:6). Henry similarly referenced the Bible other places in the speech as well. The fact that this speech was so well received and had such impact upon the Virginia legislature evidences how acceptable it was to introduce God's Word into politics during this time. And while it is possible that some may have objected, the majority must have been quite comfortable with this level of scriptural infusion. They certainly would need the comfort of the Bible in the coming days.

Patrick Henry
by George Bagby Matthews, ca. 1891.
Public Domain.

"Is life so dear, or peace so sweet, as to be purchased at the price of chains and slavery? Forbid it, Almighty God! I know not what course others may take; but as for me, give me liberty or give me death!"

– Patrick Henry

Patrick Henry was known as a fiery orator and best known was the speech he made in the House of Burgesses on March 23, 1775, in Saint John's Church in Richmond, Virginia. Henry has been credited by some historians as the force behind the Virginia House decision to mobilize for military action against the encroaching British military force.

On April 18 General Thomas Gage of the British army sent out troops to seize and destroy the weapons that he believed the colonial militia, called "minutemen," to have been stockpiling at Concord. In a story well known to most Americans, Paul Revere and William Dawes rode on horseback at night through the countryside heralding the news that the British troops were on the way. This allowed time for the minutemen to assemble. Then, sometime on the morning of the 19th, the minutemen and the British troops confronted one another. Shortly thereafter "the shot heard round the world" began the Battles of Lexington and Concord, as well as the American War of Independence, commonly known as the Revolutionary War. The colonies, Great Britain, and the world, would never be the same again.

The Second Continental Congress Convenes

When the Second Continental Congress convened on May 10, 1775, this time an unofficial delegate from Georgia was present; later, official Georgian delegates would arrive. At the forefront was the conflict in which the colonies were presently engaged. Many of the same delegates from the First Continental Congress returned. Two notable new arrivals were John Hancock, who would soon be elected president of the Congress, and Benjamin Franklin. Charles Thompson was re-elected secretary. Once again it was voted to have the Rev. Jacob Duché open with prayer.

Because war between the colonies and Britain had already commenced, Congress acted quickly to establish a regular army (June 14, 1775). Sixteen days later, Congress adopted the Articles of War, which took steps to ensure that morality prevailed within the Continental Army. Article 2 "earnestly recommended to all officers and soldiers to attend divine services." Those who behaved "indecently or irreverently" in churches would be liable to courts-martial, fines, or imprisonment.[lvi]

Although a rupture between the colonies and Britain seemed inevitable, Congress decided to appeal to King George and Parliament one more time before they pursued complete independence. Thus, a committee was appointed to draft a document titled "A Declaration by the Representatives of the United Colonies of North-America, Now Met in Congress at Philadelphia, Setting Forth the Causes and necessity of Their Taking Up Arms." John Rutledge, William Livingston, Benjamin Franklin, John Jay, and Thomas Johnson were appointed to the committee. However, Congress was not satisfied with their work, so John Dickinson and Thomas Jefferson were added to the committee as well. Dickinson and Jefferson worked together and formed a new draft, which was adopted as read on July 6. This declaration, sometimes called the "Olive Branch Petition," requested that the offensive measures against the colonies be lifted; otherwise, the colonists would fight for their liberty.

In the course of the Olive Branch Petition, God is referenced numerous times as "divine Author," "Creator," Providence," "God," and "Judge and Ruler of the Universe." Also, the drafters unequivocally specified the original purpose of America: civil and religious freedom.

> Our forefathers, inhabitants of the island of Great-Britain, left their native land, to seek on these shores a residence for civil and religious freedom.[lvii]

King George did not accept the extended olive branch. Instead, on August 23, he issued a "Proclamation of Rebellion," which declared the colonies to be in "open and avowed rebellion." Further, British officers and loyal subjects were to "exert their utmost endeavours to suppress such rebellion, and to bring the traitors to justice."[lviii] The gauntlet had been laid down: Britain would not allow the colonies their liberty without a fight.

King George III
by Sir William Beechey.
Public Domain.

Declaration of Independence

Congress did not rush toward independence. Instead, it took deliberate, time-consuming, steps and measures. At the same time, relations between Congress and Parliament continued to crumble and deteriorate. By May 1776, Congress believed it to be in order to invoke the help of God. On May 16, Congress proclaimed the following day to be one "of Humiliation, Fasting, and Prayer." Colonists were prompted to "confess and bewail our manifold sins and transgressions, and by a sincere repentance and amendment of life, appease his righteous displeasure, and through the merits and mediation of Jesus Christ, to obtain his pardon and forgiveness."[lix] Certainly this act was reflective of the Bible, where on numerous occasions, men, women, and nations fasted in times of adversity. Moreover, Congress would issue additional fast day proclamations in 1779 and 1782.[lx]

Writing the Declaration of Independence, 1776
by Jean–Leon Gerome Ferris, ca. 1863.
Public Domain.

On June 7, 1776, Richard Henry Lee introduced what might become the most important resolution ever made in Congress. Part of Lee's motion stated:

> That these United Colonies are, and of right ought to be, free and independent States, that they are absolved from all allegiance to the British Crown, and that all political connection between them and the State of Great Britain is, and ought to be, totally dissolved.[lxi]

This motion was seconded by John Adams. Yet, a vote on the resolution did not come quickly, for the vote was postponed at least three times. During this time, much politicking was done. And while the matter was quite complicated, the fundamental issue was this: Maryland, Delaware, Pennsylvania, New Jersey, New York, and South Carolina were not yet ready to sever their relationships with Great Britain. However, on July 2, the resolution finally passed. Congress had displayed foresight by appointing a committee, on June 11, to begin work on a Declaration of Independence, in the event that the resolution would pass. Thomas Jefferson, John Adams, Benjamin Franklin, Roger Sherman, and Robert Livingston were chosen to prepare the declaration. Congress realized that a bare-bones resolution stating their independence was not enough. What they needed was a fully-orbed document that convincingly stated their reasons for independence, in order to rally the colonies around the cause of independence.

Thomas Jefferson became the principal author of the Declaration. His name had appeared first in the list of committee appointees, indicating that he was the chairperson, and thus was responsible for preparing the committee's report. He had been appointed to this honorable position because of his abilities as a thinker and writer. After all, this would be a document for the ages; it required the best talent the colonies could provide.

God is referenced four times in the declaration as "Nature's God," "Creator," "Supreme Judge of the World," and "Providence." While no mention is made to Jesus Christ or Christianity, the Triune God (Father, Son, and Holy Spirit) does appear "as each branch of government—legislator, executor, and judge—and something like a Founder. And the attitude toward God in the Declaration is as the source of perfection, or rather perfection itself."[lxii] The Declaration "celebrates the blessings that come directly from God and are known through the reason with which He created us."[lxiii] It further draws upon the Bible, promoting principles of life and human dignity.

Leading up to the American War of Independence, many ministers in colonial America made the case for independence from Great Britain. At times they—and the Founding Fathers who sat under their ministries—violated hermeneutical principles, marshaling verses speaking of spiritual freedom to mean civil freedom (verses such as 2 Corinthians 3:17, Galatians 5:1 and 13, and John 8:32). However, numbers realized—following thinkers such as Samuel Rutherford (1600–1661) and John Locke (1632–1704)—that occasions do exist when resistance to civil government is justifiable. In his work Lex Rex, "Rutherford suggested that there are three appropriate levels of resistance: first, he must defend himself by protest (in contemporary society this would most often be by legal action); second, he must flee if at all possible; third, he may use force, if necessary, to defend himself."[lxiv] To those residing in colonial America, fleeing was hardly possible. And, as has been shown throughout this chapter, the Continental Congress endeavored on multiple occasions to protest Great Britain's abuse of the rights granted in the British constitution and the colonial charters. Thus, all they were left with was resistance by force. "Great Britain, because of its policy toward the colonies, was seen as a foreign power invading America. The colonists defended their homeland. As such, the American Revolution was a conservative counter-revolution. The colonists saw the British as the revolutionaries trying to overthrow the legitimate colonial governments."[lxv]

"The Founding Fathers, in the spirit of Lex Rex, cautioned in the Declaration of Independence that established governments should not be altered or abolished for 'light and transient causes.' But when there is a 'long train of abuses and usurpations' designed to produce an oppressive, authoritarian state, 'it is their right, it is their duty, to throw off such government . . .' Simply put, the Declaration of Independence states that the people, if they find that their basic rights are being systematically attacked by the state, have a duty to try to change that government, and if they cannot do so, to abolish it."[lxvi]

However, not all Americans believed that resistance to Great Britain was biblical. Some taught that Christians must be obedient and submit to governments as taught in Romans 13:1–7 and 1 Peter 2:13–17. In this position, they had the support of John Wesley, the eighteenth century British evangelist and founder of the Methodist movement. "The colonists, he wrote, 'enjoyed their liberty in a full manner as I do, or any reasonable man can desire.' Wesley listed a litany of colonial sins: they refused to pay their taxes, they had destroyed property ('Ship-loads of tea'), and most importantly, they held African slaves even as they cried for their own freedom from English tyranny. For Wesley, the cry 'no taxation without representation' was absurd: 'I reply, they are now taxed by themselves, in the very same sense that nine-tenths of us are. We have not only no vote in parliament, but none in electing the members.' Lack of representation in Parliament did not mean the colonists were exempted from 'subjection to the government and laws.'"[lxvii] To Wesley, American independence and the corresponding war was unjustifiable.

On July 4, after Congress had adopted the Declaration of Independence, it appointed Benjamin Franklin, John Adams, and Thomas Jefferson to "be a committee, to bring in a device for a seal for the United States of America."[lxviii] "Franklin's proposal adapted the biblical story of the parting of the Red Sea. Jefferson first recommended the 'Children of Israel in the Wilderness, led by a Cloud by Day, and a Pillar of Fire by night. . . .' He then embraced Franklin's proposal and rewrote it. Jefferson's revision of Franklin's proposal was presented by the committee to Congress on August 20. Although not accepted, these drafts reveal the religious temper of the Revolutionary period. Franklin and Jefferson were among the most theologically liberal of the Founders, yet they used biblical imagery for this important task."[lxix]

Articles of Confederation

When it appeared that Congress might pass a Declaration of Independence, it was "Resolved, That a committee be appointed to prepare and digest the form of a confederation to be entered into between these colonies."[lxx] During the long span in which Congress worked on the Articles, the delegates had to iron

Signing of Declaration of Independence
by Armand-Dumaresq, ca.1873.
Public Domain.

out if whether or not the colonies would have equal votes. Benjamin Franklin submitted that states' votes should be in proportion to their population, an argument not appreciated by the smaller states. He then proceeded to draw from history to support his argument, mentioning that at the time of England and Scotland's union, Scotland had made the same objection the smaller states were now making. According to Franklin, Scotland had predicted that, "it would happen again as in times of old that the whale would swallow Jonas" but instead, "Jonas had swallowed the whale."[lxxi]

First drafted in 1777, the Articles of Confederation would not be signed until 1778, and would not be ratified until March 1, 1781. The Articles would stay in force until replaced by the U.S. Constitution on March 4, 1789. "Ultimately, the Articles of Confederation [would prove to be] unwieldy and inadequate to resolve the issues that faced the United States in its earliest years . . ."[lxxii] However, this document would provide an important step in transitioning the colonies from British control to a confederation in which federal powers were granted to a central authority.[lxxiii]

About a month after the Articles of Confederation were drafted, Congress set aside a day of thanksgiving whereby the American people could "express the grateful feelings of their hearts and consecrate themselves to the service of their divine benefactor" and "join the penitent confession of their manifold sins . . . that it may please God, through the merits of Jesus Christ, mercifully to forgive and blot them out of remembrance." It was also recommended that Americans petition God "to prosper the means of religion for the promotion and enlargement of the kingdom which consisteth in righteousness, peace and joy in the Holy Ghost."[lxxiv] To those familiar with Scripture, it is obvious that the last quoted portion of the Congressional Thanksgiving Day Proclamation was drawn from Romans 14:17– "For the kingdom of God is not meat and drink; but righteousness, and peace, and joy in the Holy Ghost."

The War Ends

Following the Battle of Yorktown, British commander Lord Charles Cornwallis sent General George Washington a letter requesting terms of surrender on October 17, 1781. Two days later, Cornwallis's army surrendered to Washington.

Surrender of Lord Cornwallis
by John Trumbull, ca. 1820.
Public Domain.

On September 3, 1783, the Treaty of Paris—which began "In the name of the Most Holy and Undivided Trinity"—was signed by one British and three American ambassadors.[lxxv] Signing on behalf of the United States were John Adams, Benjamin Franklin, and John Jay, who signed their names in alphabetical order. This treaty formally ended the American War of Independence and recognized the United States of America as an independent nation. Congress ratified the treaty on January 14, 1784.

Nine days after the Treaty of Paris was signed, Congress approved a proclamation that gave God thanks for victory over Great Britain. The proclamation recommended that December 13, 1783, be set aside "to confess our manifold sins; to offer up our most fervent supplications to the God of all grace, that it may please Him to pardon our offences, and incline our hearts for the future to keep all his laws . . ."[lxxvi] Of course God's laws are recorded in the Bible, the same place where one finds the expression "God of all grace" (1 Peter 5:10), which was quoted in the proclamation.

The Constitution

To say that the Articles of Confederation had some shortcomings would be an understatement. First, each state had equal representation despite its population. Then, there was no executive, such as a president; therefore, Congress not only had to make the laws, it also had to carry them out, plus serve as a federal judiciary. To add to this already cumbersome arrangement, the states were still separate, sovereign entities that had the ability to say no to Congress. For example, states could reject requests for money. This posed a serious problem, especially since Congress had been saddled with over $50 million in debts from the war.

At first Congress attempted to improve the Articles of Confederation, but this effort soon failed. Therefore, a Constitutional Convention was convened for the purpose of constructing a new form of government. Meeting May through September 1787, the delegates worked on crafting a constitution. James Madison played a central role in the process, earning him the designation of "Father of the Constitution." The Constitution was ratified in 1788 and became effective March 4, 1789.

The Constitution primarily defined three co-equal branches of government, with checks and balances; articulated the authority of the federal government over the states; and enumerated the liberties of its citizens. Its main features, according to government scholar Larry P. Arnn, are representation, limited government, and separation of powers.[lxxvii]

While Congress was still in the thralls of heated debate over the Constitution, Benjamin Franklin recommended that a prayer be said each day. He prefaced his recommendation thus:

> I have lived, Sir, a long time; and the longer I live, the more convincing proofs I see of this truth, that God governs in the affairs of men! And if a sparrow cannot fall to the ground without his notice, is it probable that an empire can rise without his aid? We have been assured, Sir, in the sacred writings, that 'except the Lord build the house, they labor in vain that build it'. I firmly believe this; and I also believe that without his concurring aid, we shall succeed in this political building no better than the builders of Babel: we shall be confounded and we ourselves shall become a reproach and a byword down to future ages. And what is worse, mankind may hereafter, from this unfortunate instance, despair of establishing government by human wisdom, and leave it to chance, war, and conquest.[lxxviii]

Franklin demonstrated quite a familiarity with Scripture, quoting from or alluding to Daniel 4:14, Matthew 10:29, Psalm 127:1, Genesis 11:9, and Deuteronomy 28:37 (also see parallel passages to Deuteronomy 28:27—1 Kings 9:7, 2 Chronicles 7:20, Job 17:6, Job 30:9, and Psalm 44:14).

The U.S. Constitution—the longest surviving written constitution in all of history—is an extension of the Declaration. "The Founders understood the documents to be connected, to supply together the principles and the details of government, to be a persuasive and durable unity."[lxxix] Therefore, as he was in the Declaration, God is seen in the Constitution in the divisions of power—in the legislative, judicial, and executive branches.

Finally, the last action of the Continental Congress, on October 10, 1788, was to set aside land for a capital, a city that would become known as Washington, D.C. Their work was now complete; it was up to the new Congress to take up the torch.

Scene at the Signing of the Constitution of the United States
by Howard Chandler Christy, ca. 1940.
Public Domain.

Summary

As we have seen, the Continental Congress included the Bible in nearly every facet of their work. They voted to have a minister pray; this minister, the Rev. Mr. Duché, also read from the Bible. Later, Congress would form the position of chaplain (July 9, 1776). Further, the members of Congress often quoted or alluded to Scripture in their speeches. And they did not stop with scripturally-spiced speeches, for they also referenced God and the Bible in official documents such as the Olive Branch Petition, Fast Day Proclamations, the Declaration of Independence, and the Treaty of Paris. These were the same legislators who encouraged the fledgling nation to days of prayer, fasting, and thanksgiving. This led Edward F. Humphrey to remark that the proclamations and official state papers of Congress were "so filled with Biblical phrases as to resemble Old Testament ecclesiastical documents."[lxxx] Some of the members of Congress also proposed to incorporate biblical imagery into the national seal. As we will notice in chapter 6, the members of the Second Continental Congress would even endorse the printing and sale of a Bible, the first English Bible printed in North America.

CHAPTER FOUR

THE BIBLE AND THE FOUNDING FATHERS

Historian Mark A. Noll once wrote that "it would be hard to image a nation more thoroughly biblical than the United States between the American Revolution and the Civil War."[lxxxi] Moreover, the Founders helped to make it that way. After all, it was a period of biblical literacy—even the most skeptical patriots were wont to quote the Bible, though they may not always have realized they were doing so. Political scientist Donald S. Lutz said of the Founders that "they learned the Bible; they learned it down to their fingertips."[lxxxii] Gilman Marston Ostrander mentioned:

General George Washington at Trenton by John Trumbull, ca. 1792.
Public Domain.

> The American nation had been founded by intellectuals who had accepted a worldview that was based upon Biblical authority as well as Newtonian science. They had assumed that God created the earth and all life upon it at the time of creation and had continued without change thereafter. Adam and Eve were God's final creations and all of mankind had descended from them.[lxxxiii]

As Gregg L. Frazer has perceptively pointed out, since the colonies were religious, to maintain authority and power, the Founders needed to effectively appeal in a religious manner to their constituents.[lxxxiv] For this reason, it is imperative that we do not view the Founders' quoting of the Bible as an endorsement of its inspiration, infallibility, and/or inerrancy. On the same token, the Founders' quoting of the Bible does not prove their personal orthodoxy, either. What it does demonstrate, however, is that they considered the Bible relevant to contemporary society. It was authoritative. It was applicable. It was timeless. It produced morality. And it had pervaded the colonies. For these reasons, the Founders realized the Bible's connection with their current situation, as well as the advantage that scripturally-spiced speeches could afford them. Hence, John Adams, although not an orthodox Christian, could unabashedly call the Bible "the best book in the World."[lxxxv]

> *"The highest glory of the American Revolution was this: it connected, in one indissoluble bond, the principles of civil government with the principles of Christianity."*
> - John Adams

Yes, the Founders lived in a biblical milieu. But who were they exactly? To appropriately answer this query, we must first define "Founder." Some scholars have set the bounds as one who signed the Declaration of Independence, Articles of Confederation, and/or the Constitution. Others have broadened the definition to include those "who, in the last half of the eighteen century and early nineteenth century, articulated the rights of colonists, secured independence from Great Britain, and established the new constitutional republic and its political institutions."[lxxxvi] Included in the latter category are members of the Stamp Act Congress, the Continental Congress, and members of colonial/state legislative bodies. By expanding the parameters of "founder," one multiplies the number from about 120 members to thousands. For this work, the second definition will be utilized, with one limitation: only members of the Continental Congress will be discussed.

Without being too simplistic, we will look at two categories of founders: (1) those who were inconsistent or unorthodox Christians, and (2) those who were orthodox Christians, who therefore personally embraced God's Word.

Inconsistent or Unorthodox Christian Founders

The term *unorthodox* refers to that which is not orthodox. And orthodoxy, as applied here, refers to right Christian doctrine. Right doctrine in the 1700s in America was considered to be the primary tenets of Christianity held by the major denominations in the colonies: Congregational, Baptist, Presbyterian, and Anglican/Episcopalian. Many of the founders affiliated with one or more of these denominations.[lxxxvii] For example, 47 of the 55 members of the Constitutional Convention identified with these denominations. Further, the primary tenets which established orthodoxy were belief in "the Trinity, the deity of Jesus, a God active in human affairs, original sin, the Virgin Birth, the atoning work of Christ in satisfaction for man's sins, the bodily Resurrection of Christ, eternal punishment for sin, justification by faith, and the authority of the Scriptures."[lxxxviii]

Washington as Statesman at the Constitutional Convention
by Junius Brutus Stearns, ca. 1856.
Public Domain.

Frazer has submitted that the key Founders (his term)—John Adams, Thomas Jefferson, Benjamin Franklin, James Wilson, Gouverneur Morris, James Madison, Alexander Hamilton, and George Washington—were not orthodox Christians. He refers to them as theistic rationalists. Theistic rationalism this was a hybrid system that synthesized natural religion, Christianity, and an Enlightenment emphasis on reason. In this system, reason became king. For example, anything in Scripture that was deemed unreasonable was not embraced. Because the key Founders leaned so heavily on their fallible reason, they generally discredited numerous parts of the Bible. Once the Bible was discredited, it no longer served as the rule of faith and practice. "Thus saith the Lord" was replaced with "thus saith John Locke" or "thus saith Joseph Priestly or "thus saith some other thinker." But how did these Founders arrive at their theistic rationalistic positions? Answer: mainly from the intellectual clergy and professors of the day, who had received their training in or taught at the universities, especially Harvard and Yale. "Seminary students were taught to rely upon "natural law and human reason, which tended to arouse skepticism both as to the necessity and the credibility of supernatural revelation."[lxxxix]

By 1701, Harvard had already swerved aside from orthodoxy, which led to the founding of Yale. However, Yale also followed the same course. This led British evangelist George Whitefield to observe: "As for the Universities, I believe it may be said, their Light is become Darkness, Darkness that may be felt, and is complained of by the most godly Ministers."[xc]

Combating the unorthodoxy of the age were ministers such as Whitefield and Jonathan Edwards. These two helped to spawn the Great Awakening, an American revival of the 1730s and 40s that emphasized the new birth, a personal conversion experience in which one received forgiveness of sins by God. While some historians feel the long-term effects of the Great Awakening were negligible, others believe it to be "the single most transforming event in the religious history of colonial America."[xci] Those who were the most impacted were Baptists and Methodists—groups of which none of the key Founders were part. In addition, the Great Awakening often reached poor whites, Indians, and free and enslaved blacks—groups with which the key Founders also did not identify.

The Great Awakening did not seem to influence the key founders away from their entrenched rationalism, although the ministry of men such as Whitefield did, to a small degree, touch the likes of Benjamin Franklin. The account is given of one of the occasions when Franklin went to hear Whitefield, who was raising money for an orphanage to be built in Georgia. Franklin later wrote:

> I thought it would have been better to have built the house here, and brought the children to it. This I advis'd; but he . . . rejected my counsel, and I therefore refus'd to contribute. I happened soon after to attend one of his sermons, in the course of which I perceived he intended to finish with a collection, and I silently resolved he should get nothing from me. I had in my pocket a handful of copper money, three or four silver dollars, and five pistoles in gold. As he proceeded I began to soften, and concluded to give the coppers. Another stroke of his oratory made me asham'd of that, and determin'd me to give the silver; and he finish'd so admirably, that I empty'd my pocket wholly into the collector's dish, gold and all.[xcii]

Franklin at the Constitutional Convention 1787 by Joseph Boggs Beale, ca. 1880–1900.
Public Domain.

Now we will briefly note two inconsistent or unorthodox Christian Founders, especially their positions in respect to the Bible. These two are part of the group Frazer refers to as "key Founders." Later we will explore two orthodox Christian Founders.

George Washington

Historian Edwin S. Gaustad made the following observation:

> The last decade of the eighteen century found Americans searching for a center. Once that center had been located in loyalty to England and the monarchy, but this loyalty could no longer unify. Later that center had been the military effort required to overthrow Britain's army and navy, but the Revolution had now ended.[xciii]

Gaustad went on to posit that Americans found a center in two men: Benjamin Franklin and George Washington. We now will turn our focus to the latter.

George Washington served as a member of the Continental Congress but was catapulted to national recognition for his role in the American War of Independence,

The March to Valley Forge
by William B. T. Trego, ca. 1883
Public Domain.

having served as general and commander in chief of the Continental Army. Following the War, Washington later served as the president of the Constitutional Convention, and affixed his name to the U.S. Constitution. Of course, Washington was elected first president of the United States of America, garnering him the title, "Father of the Country." As Henry Lee observed, Washington was "first in war, first in peace, first in the hearts of his countrymen." Lee further commented that "vice shuddered" in Washington's presence and that "the purity of his private character gave effulgence to his public virtues."[xciv]

Washington's inauguration as president notably incorporated at least seven religious activities:

    (1) The use of the Bible to administer the oath

    (2) The inclusion of "So help me God!" to the oath

    (3) Prayers offered by the president

    (4) Religious content to the inaugural address

    (5) Civil leaders calling the nation to prayer or acknowledgment of God

    (6) Inaugural worship services attended en masse by Congress as an official part of congressional activities

    (7) Clergy-led inaugural prayers.

Concerning religion, Washington stated that his "tenets were few and simple."[xcv] In addition, he possessed the ability to remain aloof above religious controversies, winning him the respect of most American Christians, Protestant and Catholic alike. His was something of a generic faith—one which identified somewhat with Christianity, yet not completely. For example, Washington was wont to refer to God as "Heaven," "Almighty Being," "Governor of the Universe," "Higher Cause," "Great Ruler of Events," "the Supreme Dispenser of all Good," "the Supreme being," "the Supreme Ruler of the Universe," "the Supreme Ruler of nations," "Sovereign Arbiter of Nations," "great disposer of human Events," "interposing Hand of Heaven," "All Wise Creator," "parent of the human race," "Maker," and the "Divine Author of life"—designations that all fell short of expressing belief in Jesus Christ as God. This does not indicate per se that Washington was not an orthodox Christian, for in using a "multitude of respectful titles for God, he was simply employing a Baroque style popular among many of the ministers at the time."[xcvi] What is concerning, however, is his dearth of direct references to Jesus Christ, references also made by the ministers at the time.

Yet, Washington was no deist. He did not believe that God was a watchmaker who had "wound the world up and retired." Instead he saw God active and intervening in the affairs of men.[xcvii] Thus he often referred to God as "Providence" (some 270 times).[xcviii] Frazer counted 57 letters, addresses, or public documents in which Washington referred to God's involvement in the fledgling nation (he also cites only one mention of Jesus Christ in 20,000 pages of Washington's writings.)[xcix] Washington also believed in prayer and at times requested Congress and the nation to join him in imploring God. He reported praying "humbly," "fervently," and "earnestly."[c] Incidentally the Bible uses the terms "humble" and "earnest" to describe elements of true prayer (2 Chronicles 7:14; James 5:16)

Although Washington promoted Christian morals and behavior in others, he at times desecrated the Sabbath (transacting business and going fox hunting instead of attending church) and did not receive communion for a period of time. Washington's adopted granddaughter, Nelly Custis, lends her support here, stating: "On communion Sundays he left the church with me, after the blessing, and returned home, and we sent the carriage back for grandmother."[ci] Dr. James Abercrombie, assistant rector of Christ Church, where Washington sometimes attended in Philadelphia, acknowledged that Washington was "a professing Christian." Yet, he confided, "Truth requires me to say, that General Washington never received the communion, in the churches of which I am parochial Minister." Abercrombie also had to confess, "I cannot consider any man as a real Christian who uniformly disregards an ordinance so solemnly enjoined by the divine Author of our holy religion, and considered as a channel of divine grace."[cii] In addition, Washington rarely, if ever, clearly articulated faith in Jesus Christ, even when others specifically endeavored to get him to do such. The closest he came was an oath he took in a private letter in which he wrote, "on my honor and the faith of a Christian."[ciii] Most of the time, if not all of the time, Washington spoke of Christians in the third person.[civ] However, Washington professed to be a Christian. Nelly Custis once wrote that "General Washington avowed himself to me to be a believer in Christianity."[cv] As commander and chief of the Continental Army, he gave a soldier a Christian burial.[cvi] He also had a vital interest in the evangelization of the Indians and even consented to assist Selina, Countess of Huntington (Lady Huntington) in such an effort.[cvii] Furthermore, the stone placed on Washington's crypt reads:

I am the resurrectionand the life, saith the Lord
he that believeth in me, though he were dead, yet shall he live;
and whosoever liveth and believeth in me shall never die
St John, XI:25.26

So was George Washington a Christian? Ultimately, we are not the arbiters of that question. However, based upon historical evidence, we observe that Washington at times identified with Christianity, professed Christianity, served as a vestryman and churchwarden, and even lent his support to the evangelization of the Indians to Christianity. In addition, he evidenced belief in a number of the tenets of orthodoxy. Yet, he also at times fell short of a strict observance of Christianity and did not express his Christian faith often, if at all. Therefore a careful analysis of Washington leads us to view our first president as a professed Christian who sometimes fell short of practicing true Christianity. This assessment is not too strong, for the Bible is clear that Christians should take communion (1 Corinthians 11:23–26), should openly declare their faith (Psalm 107:2; Mark 8:38; Luke 9:26; Acts 10:42; Revelation 12:11), and should not desecrate the Sabbath (Exodus 20:8; 31:14–15; Leviticus 9:3, 30; 26:2; Deuteronomy 5:12; Hebrews 10:25).

When it comes to the Bible, Washington appears to have held some or full belief in written revelation, once writing that "above all, the pure and benign light of Revelation" predicated "the blessings of society."[cviii] Further, he referenced the Bible as the "Word of God," "Scripture," and "Holy Writ," although he never specifically articulated whether or not the Bible was infallible.[cix] He quoted both humorously and seriously from the Bible, borrowing "scriptural phrases and concepts from all parts of the Bible."[cx]

Washington's favorite verse was Micah 4:4—"But they shall sit every man under his vine and under his fig tree; and none shall make them afraid: for the mouth of the LORD of hosts hath spoken it." Throughout his correspondence he alluded to or quoted this verse more than 40 times, often in connection to his retiring to Mount Vernon. To underscore how familiar Washington was with Scripture, below is the body of a short letter he wrote to Marquis de Lafayette on July 25, 1785.

> As the clouds which overspread your hemisphere are dispersing, and peace with all its concomitants is dawning upon your Land, I will banish the sound of War from my letter: I wish to see the sons and daughters of the world in Peace and busily employed in the more agreeable amusement of fulfilling the first and great commandment, Increase and Multiply: as an encouragement to which we have opened the fertile plains of the Ohio to the poor, the needy and the oppressed of the Earth; any one therefore who is heavy laden, or who wants land to cultivate, may repair thither and abound, as in the Land of promise, with milk and honey: the ways are preparing, and the roads will be made easy, thro' the channels of Potomac and James river.[cxi]

Peter A. Lillback correctly points out that in this short letter there are no fewer than seven allusions to Scripture:

> (1) first and great commandment (Matthew 22:38)
> (2) Increase and Multiply (Genesis 1:28)
> (3) to the poor, the needy (Deuteronomy 24:14)
> (4) heavy laden (Matthew 11:28)
> (5) Land of promise (Exodus 12:25)
> (6) with milk and honey (Exodus 3:8)
> (7) ways are preparing (Isaiah 40:3).[cxii]

Washington possessed some important editions of the Bible, including a Theodore Beza Latin Bible and a Bishop's Bible. He also became a subscriber of Brown's Self-Interpreting Bible.[cxiii] This meant that Washington paid for his Bible in advance, so as to make the project possible. Near the end of the war, he supported the idea of giving each soldier a Bible.

More important, Washington would read a chapter to his family before they went to church on Sunday, a fact recorded by Washington's personal secretary Tobias Lear.[cxiv] Thus we see a definite connection between the Bible and one of the most distinguished members to have ever served in Congress.

The Washington Family
by Edward Savage in stages
from 1789 to 1796.
Public Domain.

Thomas Jefferson

Thomas Jefferson started in politics at an early age, being elected to Virginia's House of Burgesses while still in his twenties. Afterward he served in the Continental Congress, most notably being the chief author of the Declaration of Independence. He later had the privilege of signing the very instrument into which he had poured so much of his intellectual energy and patriotism. Later, Jefferson was appointed by Washington to serve as the nation's first Secretary of State. Finally, his two terms as the third president of the United States of America would cap a lifetime of governmental service.

From his youth, Jefferson developed a fascination with religion, a fascination that would extend to his death. He once shared: "I never go to bed without an hour, or half an hour's previous reading of something moral."[cxv]

In fact, he believed his authoring of the Virginia Statute for Religious Freedom to be one of his greatest achievements. He corresponded much, exploring questions involving religion and theology. Thus, Jefferson biographer Edwin Gaustad could refer to Jefferson as "the most self-consciously theological of all American presidents."[cxvi]

In regards to religion, Jefferson personally claimed to be a Christian, describing his belief system as "rational Christianity."[cxvii] "He stated that he was conversant with and an adherent to the 'doctrines' of 'the unlettered Apostles, the Apostolic fathers, and the Christians of the 1st century."[cxviii] He also claimed to hold to the "doctrines of Jesus" and "the genuine precepts of Jesus."[cxix] He testified, "I am a real Christian, that is to say, a disciple of the doctrines of Jesus."[cxx] However—as we will notice later—Jefferson's professions of Christianity did not equate to orthodox Christianity.

Declaration of Independence
by John Trumbull, ca. 1819.
Public Domain.

Jefferson, like Washington, was no deist, for he too recognized the God of creation, regularly referring to "the Creator" and the "wise creator." He even argued for a Creator God based upon the first three verses of the Gospel of John, demonstrating a degree of belief in the authority of Scripture. He also maintained that God was active in human affairs. Once, when writing to John Adams, Jefferson stated that it was "impossible for the human mind not to perceive and feel a conviction of design, consummate skill, and indefinite power in every atom of its composition."[cxxi]

Jefferson—also unlike a deist—believed in prayer. That is why he suggested in 1774 that Virginia set a day apart for fasting, humiliation and prayer. Acting upon Jefferson's suggestion, the House of Burgesses adopted a resolution on May 24 to set June 1 apart for such. Also, Jefferson never claimed to be a deist, speaking of deists in the third person.

Although Jefferson claimed to hold to the "doctrines of Jesus" he failed the orthodoxy test at several points. For example, he rejected plenary (full) inspiration of the Bible, the incarnation, the deity of Jesus, the Trinity, the atonement, justification by faith, eternal punishment for sin, and the resurrection. Yet, unlike deists, Jefferson placed Jesus Christ on a pedestal, contending that he was the best

Jefferson's Monticello

William Cullen Bryan and Sydney Howard Gay, *A Popular History of the United States* (New York: Charles Scribners' Sons, 1881).
Public Domain.

human personification of morals and ethics. He stated: "Of all the systems of morality, ancient or modern, which have come under my observation, none appear to me so pure as that of Jesus."[cxxii] Yet, Jefferson did not believe that Jesus Christ was truly God. Herein Jefferson's logic was flawed, for Jesus is either God as He claimed to be (Mark 14:62; John 1:8; 3:16; 5:32; 8:24, 58; 10:30) or He is a liar or lunatic, and therefore no example of morals and ethics.

In wrestling with this dilemma, Jefferson attempted to take a middle-of-the-road approach: he contended that Jesus never claimed to be God. In doing so, Jefferson missed the very center of Christianity: Jesus Christ—fully God, fully man—who made atonement for the sins of mankind. Thus it was only natural for Jefferson to believe that all roads led to God and to dismiss Jesus' claim: "I am the way, the truth, and the life: no man cometh unto the Father, but by me" (John 14:6). Instead of accepting Jesus as the only road to Heaven, Jefferson stated:

> Let us not be uneasy then about the different roads we may pursue, as believing them the shortest, to that our last abode; but, following the guidance of a good conscience, let us be happy in the hope that by these different paths we shall all meet in the end.[cxxiii]

Even Joseph Priestly—a prominent Unitarian minister, scientist, and friend of Jefferson—worried that Jefferson was not genuinely a Christian.[cxiv] This is certainly insightful, since Jefferson had written to John Adams concerning Priestly: "I have read his Corruptions of Christianity, and Early opinions of Jesus, over and over again; and I rest them . . . as the basis of my own faith."[cxxv]

Jefferson had a large interest in the Bible, partly evidenced by the tens of Bibles that were part of his library.[cxxvi] He used these Bibles in his critical analysis of Scripture, an analysis strongly influenced by rationalism. Jefferson said of the Old Testament that "the whole of history of these books is so defective and doubtful that it seems vain to attempt minute enquiry into it."[cxxvii] He referenced "dunghills in the New Testament.[cxxviii] He counseled someone to read the Bible critically, "as you would Livy or Tacitus."[cxxix] Further, he referred to the Book of Revelation as "the ravings of a Maniac, no more worthy, nor capable of explanation than the incoherences of our nightly dreams."[cxxx]

Jefferson's hang-up with the Bible could be summarized thus: he rested too much on reason, and too often excluded faith. Hence, he struggled with miracles and Jesus' provision of redemption through His death on the cross.[cxxxi] Jefferson ultimately failed to realize and embrace the Bible's emphasis on faith. Notably, the Bible stresses that "without faith it is impossible to please [God]" (Hebrews 11:6) and also states that "the just shall live by faith: but if any man draw back, my soul shall have no pleasure in him" (Hebrews 10:38).

Jefferson's study into the Bible led him to compile *The Life and Morals of Jesus*, his reconstruction of the Gospels. He began this project while president, although he did not complete it until 1820, at the age of 77.[cxxxii] Jefferson cut out passages of the Gospels in four different languages—English, French, Latin, and Greek—and arranged them into what he believed to be a chronological order. "He then pasted the extracts he had chosen on blank pages of paper, laying them in four columns across the pages so as to allow immediate comparison among the different language versions of each Bible verse. When finished, he sent his pages to a Richmond bookbinder, who stitched them together in a red leather binding adorned with gold tooling."[cxxxiii] Only one such book was bound. He wrote to John Adams, "I have performed this operation for my own use."[cxxxiv]

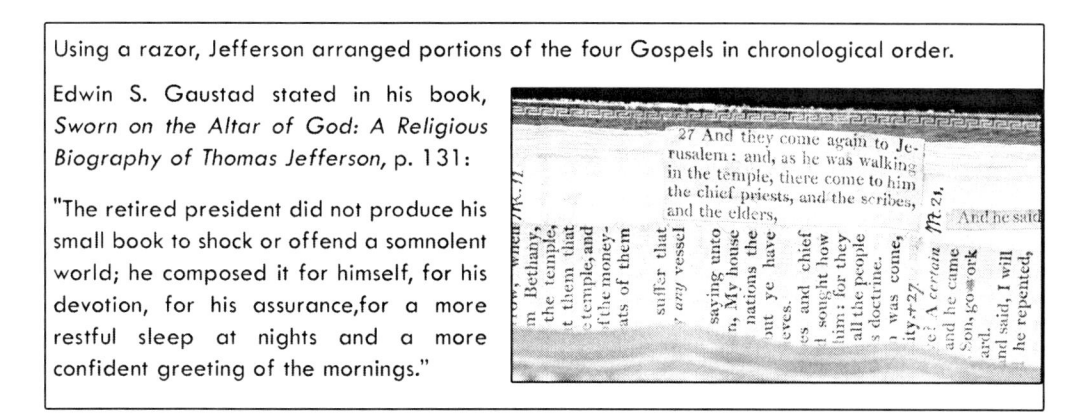

Using a razor, Jefferson arranged portions of the four Gospels in chronological order.

Edwin S. Gaustad stated in his book, *Sworn on the Altar of God: A Religious Biography of Thomas Jefferson*, p. 131:

"The retired president did not produce his small book to shock or offend a somnolent world; he composed it for himself, for his devotion, for his assurance, for a more restful sleep at nights and a more confident greeting of the mornings."

Jefferson's *The Life and Morals* of Jesus, later known as Jefferson's Bible, was not simply a polyglot harmony (a chronological arrangement of the Gospels in multiple languages). Instead, it was an attempt to rid the Gospels of anything that Jefferson considered to be "contrary to reason."[cxxxv] "Absent are the annunciation, the resurrection, the water being turned to wine, and the multitudes fed on five loaves of bread and two fishes."[cxxxvi] The last verse of the Jefferson Bible reads: "There laid they Jesus, and they rolled a great stone to the door of the sepulcher, and departed." The finished product illustrates Jefferson's disbelief of the Bible's inspiration, infallibility, and inerrancy. This proof alone is enough to demonstrate that Thomas Jefferson was not an orthodox Christian. Besides that, the Jefferson Bible also demonstrates Jefferson's disbelief in the deity and resurrection of Jesus. Jefferson himself once stated: "I am of a sect by myself, as far as I know."[cxxxvii]

In 1902, Congressman John F. Lacey of Iowa introduced a resolution for Congress to print a facsimile of the Jefferson Bible. This resolution was passed by both houses and the project was assigned to the Government Printing Office. Each page of the Jefferson Bible was carefully photographed, and in 1904 the third president's *The Life and Morals of Jesus was* published for the first time, with 9,000 copies delivered to Congress. "In following years, newly elected senators each received a copy of the book on the day they swore their oath of office, a tradition that did not end until the books ran out in the 1950s."[cxxxviii] Notably, in 2011 the Smithsonian Institution published the first full-color facsimile of the Jefferson Bible.

Life and Morals of Jesus
Image from 1902 Facsimile.
Public Domain.

Orthodox Christian Founders

John Jay

John Jay began his career in politics upon his election to a New York committee tasked with the responsibility of suppressing violence incited by some of the states' more radical patriots. Later, Jay served New York by drafting the first constitution of New York, serving as the state's chief justice, and at the end of his political career, serving as governor, having been elected while he was in Great Britain. On a more national level, Jay was twice elected to the Continental Congress, serving as the body's president from December 10, 1778 to September 28, 1779. John Jay, along with John Adams and Benjamin Franklin, signed the Treaty of Paris, which officially ended the American War of Independence. He authored five of the Federalist Papers and had the prominence of being appointed by Washington as the first chief justice of the United States Supreme Court.

John Jay was unapologetically an orthodox Christian. He once wrote: "I have long been of opinion that the Evidence of the Truth of Christianity requires only to be carefully examined to produce conviction in candid minds."[cxxxix] Once, upon being challenged concerning his faith by atheists in France, Jay responded "that I did [believe], and that I thanked God that I did."[cxl]

John Jay
by Gilbert Stuart, ca. 1794.
Public Domain.

Jay was a devoted student of the Bible, especially prophecy. This led John Adams to write to Thomas Jefferson that he worried that his son, John Quincy, would "retire like Jay to study Prophecies to the End of his Life."[cxli]

David L. Holmes noted that John Jay used designations for God such as "Providence," "Creator," and "Divine Providence."

> But most of his language was that commonly used in the orthodox Protestant circles of his time: "Savior," "King of Heaven," "Author and Giver of the Gospel," "Lord of the Sabbath," "Almighty God," "Lord of Hosts," "Almighty and benevolent Being," "Master," and "Captain of our Salvation." In addition, Jay used Christian terms that would rarely turn up in the writings of a founding father: "gospel," "gospel ministry," "mercy," "grace," "divine ordinances," and "apostolic succession."[cxlii]

Throughout his writings, Jay demonstrated a familiarity with the Bible. For example, one of his letters referenced Moses, Paul, Solomon, David and Absalom, the Last Supper, Peter, and John the Baptist. In addition, he was not reticent to include religious language in his public addresses.

At home, Jay was mindful of rearing his family in Christianity. He encouraged his son Peter Augustus: "The Bible is the best of all Books, for it is the word of God, and teaches us the way to be happy in his world and in the next. Continue therefore to read it, and to regulate your Life by its precepts."[cxliii] He wrote to his other children, challenging them to prepare their souls for the world to come. "When Jay's wife died, his immediate response was to take the family into the other room, read I Corinthians 15 on Christian resurrection, and lead them in prayers."[cxliv] After his daughter Sarah Louisa died he remarked, "The removal of my excellent daughter from the house of her earthly, to the house of her Heavenly Father, leaves me nothing to regret or lament on her account. . . . This temporary separation will terminate in a perpetual reunion."[cxlv]

Guests witnessed the Jays "uniting in thanksgiving, confession, and prayer.[cxlvi] Timothy Dwight, who served as president of Yale, commented that Jay spent his time in "profound attention to those immense objects which ought ever supremely to engage the thoughts, wishes, and labors of an immortal being."[cxlvii]

John Jay ardently believed that God rules in the affairs of men to accomplish His will.[cxlviii] In addition, he believed that Providence had directed the founding of the United States. He wrote:

> A proper history of the United States would have much to recommend it: in some respects it would be singular, or unlike all others; it would develop the great plan of Providence, for causing this extensive part of our world to be discovered, and these "uttermost parts of the earth" to be gradually filled with civilized and Christian people and nations. The means or second causes by which this great plan has long been and still is accomplishing, are materials for history, of which the writer ought well to know the use and bearings and proper places. In my opinion, the historian, in the course of the work, is never to lose sight of that great plan.[cxlix]

John Jay felt the importance of encouraging Christian societies. He was a member of the American Board of Commissioners of Foreign Missions and supported the American Society for Educating Pious Youth for the Gospel Ministry. Yet, it was the American Bible Society (ABS) with which Jay became most active, serving as its vice president from its inception in 1816 to 1821 and serving as its president from 1821 to 1825. He believed that America's hope rested upon the Scripture and its dissemination. Concerning voluntary Christian societies like the ABS, Jay stated:

> We have reason to rejoice that such institutions have been so greatly multiplied and cherished in the United States; especially as a kind Providence has blessed us, not only with peace and plenty, but also with the full and secure enjoyment of our civil and religious rights and privileges.[cl]

Concerning the Bible, Jay told the ABS:

> The Bible will also inform them that our gracious Creator has provided for us a Redeemer, in whom all the nations of the earth shall be blessed: that this Redeemer has made atonement for the sins of the whole world, and . . . has opened a way for our redemption and salvation.[cli]

It is important to mention that the ABS's first president, Elias Boudinot, had also served in the Continental Congress—for a while as president—and later in the U.S. House of Representatives. In addition to these prominent positions, Boudinot also served as Director of the United States Mint. Boudinot was troubled at the inroads of skepticism in America and was much disturbed by the popularity of Thomas Paine's The Age of Reason (1794). To this end he poured his "considerable energies, finances, and personal connections to bind together disparate local Bible societies into one powerful, centralized group."[clii]

Jay, like Boudinot, also desired to combat unbelief with Scripture. In accepting the position of president of the ABS upon the death of Boudinot, Jay declared:

> They who regard these Societies as deriving their origin and success from the author and Giver of the Gospel, cannot forbear concluding it to be the duty of Christians, to promote the purposes for which they have been established; and that is particularly incumbent on their officers to be diligent in the business committed to them.[cliii]

John Jay, First Chief Justice
This portrait was engraved in 1863 after a painting by Alonzo Chappel.
Public Domain.

Other Founders who were members and/or officers of the ABS included:

1. James Brown (Revolutionary War soldier; Minister to France; U.S. senator)
2. DeWitt Clinton (U.S. senator; Mayor of New York City; Governor of New York)
3. Jonas Galusha (Revolutionary War soldier; Vermont State Supreme Court justice and governor)
4. William Gaston (U.S. Representative; North Carolina State Supreme Court justice)
5. Charles Goldsborough (U.S. representative; Governor of Maryland)
6. William Gray (Revolutionary War soldier; Constitution ratification delegate from Virginia)
7. Felix Grundy (U.S. representative, U.S. senator)
8. William Jones (Revolutionary War soldier; Governor of Rhode Island
9. Andrew Kirkpatrick (U.S. representative; New Jersey Supreme Court chief justice)
10. Rufus King (Revolutionary War soldier; Signer of Constitution; U.S. senator)
11. John Langdon (Delegate to Continental Congress; Signer of Constitution; U.S. senator)
12. George Madison (Revolutionary War soldier; Governor of Kentucky)
13. John Marshall (Minuteman officer; U.S. representative; Secretary of State; U.S. Supreme Court justice)
14. David Morril (U.S. senator; Governor of New Hampshire)
15. Joseph Nourse (Military secretary to General Charles Lee; Clerk/Paymaster for BoW)
16. William Phillips (Lieutenant Governor of Massachusetts; State senator)
17. Charles C. Pinckney (Revolutionary War officer; Signer of Constitution)
18. Thomas Posey (Revolutionary War officer; State and U.S. senator)
19. Isaac Shelby (Revolutionary War officer; First governor of Kentucky)
20. John Cotton Smith (U.S. representative; Connecticut Supreme Court justice; Governor of Connecticut)
21. Caleb Strong (Delegate to Constitutional Convention; U.S. senator; Governor of Massachusetts)
22. Smith Thompson (New York State Supreme Court chief justice; U.S. Supreme Court justice)
23. William Tilghman (Constitution ratification delegate from Pennsylvania; Pennsylvania Supreme Court chief justice)
24. Daniel Tompkins (New York Supreme Court justice; Vice-President under James Monroe)
25. Robert Troup (Revolutionary War Lieutenant-Colonel; New York U.S. District Court judge)
26. Peter Vroom (Governor of New Jersey; U.S. representative; New Jersey Supreme Court chief justice)
27. Bushrod Washington (Revolutionary War soldier; Constitution ratification delegate from Virginia)
28. William Wirt (Virginia State House member; U.S. Attorney; U.S. Attorney-General under James Monroe)
29. Thomas Worthington (Delegate to Constitutional Convention from Ohio; U.S. senator; Governor of Ohio)[cliv]

Contemporary with Jay and Boudinot was another patriot leader who involved himself with the Bible. Charles Thompson, "the Sam Adams of Philadelphia," had served as the secretary of the Continental Congress throughout the body's duration (1774–1789). Afterward he gave himself to translating the Septuagint (the Greek translation of the Hebrew Old Testament) into English, a project that would require some 30 years to complete. When it was published in 1808, Thompson's work achieved a first: it was the first translation of the Septuagint into English. "Although his translation garnered a great deal of respect in the scholarly community, it never enjoyed wide popular appeal."[clv]

In 1827, when John Jay lay dying, one of his children asked him on what foundation he rested his hopes and consolation. His reply was succinct: "They have the Book."[clvi] In his will, Jay wrote:

> While my children lament my departure let them recollect that in doing them good I was only the agent of their Heavenly Father, and that he never withdraws his care and consolations from those who diligently seek him.[clvii]

The epitaph upon his tombstone read: "He was in his life and death an example of the virtues, the faith and the hopes of a Christian."[clviii] Quite fittingly, he was the last member of the Continental Congress to die. He was certainly an example of a true Christian statesman, who desired to see his countrymen blessed with their own copies of God's Holy Word.

Samuel Adams

Samuel Adams became politically active around the time of the Stamp Act, a tax levied to raise revenue to provide for the defense of the colonies following the French and Indian War (1754–1763). This event spurred Adams to organize Committees of Correspondence. He then served in the Massachusetts General Court from 1765 to 1774. Afterward, Adams became a member of the Continental Congress, a body upon which he exerted a large influence from 1774 to 1781. Later he returned to Massachusetts politics, serving as president of the Massachusetts Senate in 1781, and as governor from 1794 to 1797.

Samuel Adams' role in the revolution cannot be underemphasized. He has been given such accolades as "the Man of the Revolution," and "Patriarch of Liberty" (both by Thomas Jefferson), and the "undaunted and illustrious patriot" (by the House of Representatives). Biographer Benjamin Irvin argued that, "Adams was responsible for making the Revolution happen."[clix] John Adams said that his cousin, Samuel Adams possessed "the most thorough Understanding of Liberty . . . as well as the most habitual, radical Love of it" (among the leaders of the revolutionary cause in Boston).[clx] In short, he was a Revolutionary's Revolutionary.

Since his death, Samuel Adams has been viewed through different lenses. Some have seen a troublemaker and rabble-rouser, intent on causing mischief and tumult. Others have seen a steady patriot and firebrand who championed the cause of civil and religious liberty. Those who knew Adams best often concurred with the latter sentiment. They were acquainted with a man of pious character, who

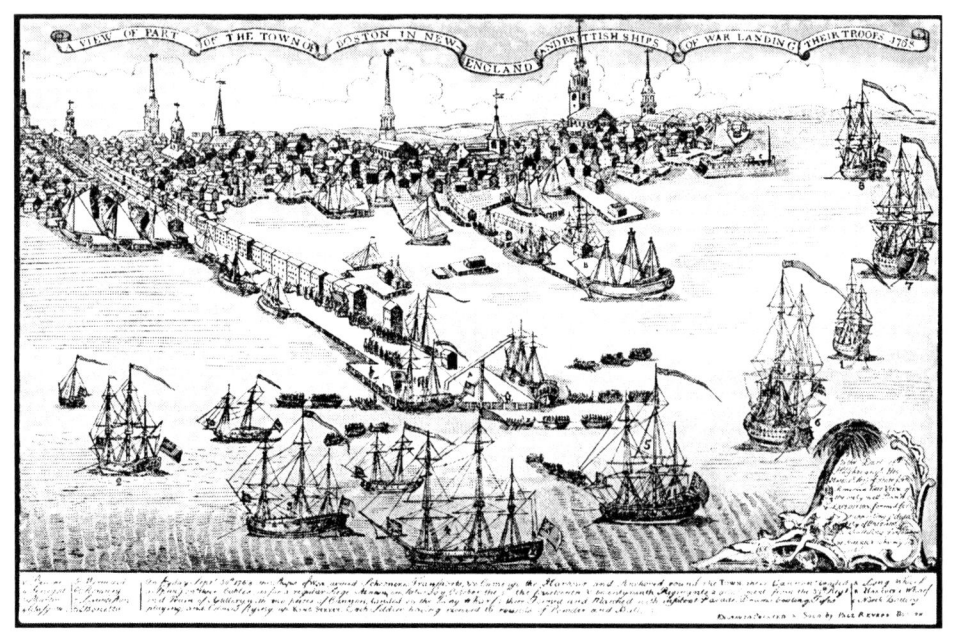

A view of the Town of Boston in New England and British Ships of War landing their troops
Reproduction of 1768 engraving by Paul Revere.
Public Domain.

sacrificed wealth and comfort to fight for freedom. According to historian John Fea, Adams is nowadays popularly perceived as a rabble-rouser who incited mob violence as a leader of the Sons of Liberty. To set the record straight— Adams was never directly connected to this group and also denounced rioting in the streets of Boston. He felt, correctly so, that such rioting often led to the unnecessary destruction of property, British or otherwise.[clxi]

Samuel Adams' personal life was shaped by his Congregational rearing and the First Great Awakening, the revival spearheaded by Jonathan Edwards and George Whitefield in the 1730s and 40s. The Great Awakening stressed the need for regeneration or the "new birth," whereby a repentant sinner believes in Christ as his or her Savior and is given spiritual life.

Theologian Jonathan Edwards
Engraved by R. Babson & J. Andrews; Print. by Wilson & Daniels, prior to 1855.
Public Domain.

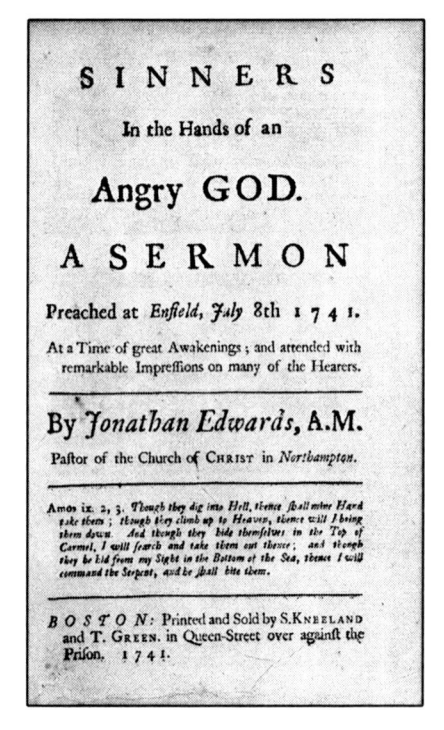

"Sinners in the Hands of An Angry God"
Sermon Preached at Enfield, July 8, 1741 by Rev. Jonathan Edwards.

The Great Awakening may have helped Adams to remain orthodox in a time when he was surrounded by rationalism. Adams unabashedly signed essays "a religious politician" and stated that his goal was "to promote the spiritual kingdom of Jesus Christ."[clxii] He even wrote in his will of his reliance "on the merits of Jesus Christ for the pardon of all my sins."[clxiii] In carrying out his faith, Adams read the Bible daily, spent personal time in prayer, strictly observed the Sabbath, attended church faithfully, prayed with his family before meals, and had devotions with his family every morning and evening.

He referred to God using generic titles, as well as by using unabashedly Christian titles such as "the common Master," "our Divine Redeemer, "Him . . . who has given us his Son to purchase for us the reward of eternal life," and "all who love the Lord Jesus Christ in sincerity."[clxiv] As governor of Massachusetts he issued a Thanksgiving proclamation mentioning "that holy and happy period when the kingdom of our Lord and Saviour Jesus Christ may be everywhere established . . ."[clxv]

Like John Jay, Samuel Adams also saw God's providential plan unfolding with the forming of the United States of America. He declared to the Continental Congress in 1777 that "numerous have been the manifestations of God's providence in sustaining us. In the gloomy period of adversity, we have had 'our cloud by day and pillar of fire by night.' "[clxvi] This was, of course, a reference to the pillar that led the Children of Israel out of Egypt and into Canaan. As we have seen earlier, the Founders were wont to compare the colonies' quest for liberty with Israel's. Further, Adams believed that the colonies possessed a God-given responsibility to withstand tyranny. In fact, he held that God would punish the colonies if they did not resist tyranny. He once wrote to his wife: "If heaven punishes Communities for their Vices, how sore must be the Punishment of that Community who thinks the Rights of human nature not worth struggling for and patiently submit to Tyranny."[clxvii]

As a politician, Adams sought to elevate the importance of morality and virtue among Americans, especially those of Massachusetts and Boston. He was troubled by those who lived for material gain and rejected Christian faith and principles.[clxviii]

He, like contemporary John Wesley in Great Britain, even led efforts to discontinue the theater, believing it promoted vice and "distracted audiences from their Christian responsibilities."[clxix] Adams was also troubled by gambling, extravagance, and wastefulness. His desire for a virtuous society is seen in a 1776 letter to John Scollay:

> I have long been convinced that our enemies have made it an Object, to eradicate from the Minds of the People in general a Sense of true Religion & Virtue, in hopes thereby the more easily to carry their Point of enslaving them. Indeed my Friend, this is a Subject so important in my Mind, that I know not how to leave it. Revelation assures us that "Righteousness exalteth a Nation"—Communities are dealt with in this World by the wise and just Ruler of the Universe. He rewards or punishes them according to their general Character. The diminution of publick Virtue is usually attended with that of publick Happiness, and the publick Liberty will not long survive the total Extinction of Morals. "The Roman Empire, says the Historian, must have sunk, though the Goths had not invaded it. Why? Because the Roman Virtue was sunk." Could I be assured that America would remain virtuous, I would venture to defy the utmost Efforts of Enemies to subjugate her. You will allow me to remind you, that the Morals of that City which has born so great a Share of the American Contest, depend much upon the Vigilance of the respectable Body of Magistrates of which you are a Member.[clxx]

Samuel Adams filled his speeches with references from Scripture, as has already been demonstrated. In addition, He once referenced King Jeroboam (introduced in 1 Kings 11:26) as a "perjur'd Traitor" who rebelled "against God and his Country."[clxxi] On another occasion he stated that clergy who promoted "excessive" compliance to the government might be guilty of "lying against the Holy Ghost," a clear reference to Acts 5:3.[clxxii]

When Adams died in 1803, he became known as "the Last of the Puritans," a designation that denoted that Adams was largely in a class of his own as a Christian statesman. Although he attended Harvard while that school was drifting away from orthodoxy, he remained orthodox. And although he worked closely with Washington, Franklin, and Jefferson, he did not allow those men's rationalism to obscure his clear view of faith. O, that we had more statesmen like Samuel Adams today!

Summary

The Founders were certainly not Bible illiterate. Instead, they evidenced a familiarity with Scripture and, in some cases, were even wont to quote it. Whether the Founders were orthodox or not mattered little when it came to their quoting of Scripture; the unorthodox quoted the Bible as did the orthodox. This points to the religious training that many of the Founders had received. It also points to the influence that religion and the Bible exercised on the colonies and infant nation.

Washington
by Gilbert Stuart,
ca. 1846.

John Jay
by Stuart/Trumbull,
ca. 1784–1818.

Thomas Jefferson
by Rembrandt Peale,
ca. 1800.

Samuel Adams
by Major John Johnston,
ca. 1795.

all four portraits are in
Public Domain.

CHAPTER FIVE

Robert Aitken's Bible

During the American War of Independence (1775–1783), Bibles for sale within the colonies became scarce, and the reason was quite simple: the war had halted importation of Bibles from the mother country.

Bibles had not been printed in the colonies prior to this time for at least a couple of reasons. First, the Authorized Version—also known as the King James Bible—was held under a royal license. This meant that only the British crown could authorize the printing of un-annotated (not possessing comments) King James Bibles. And no one in the rebellious colonies could possibly gain that authorization. Another reason that Bibles were not printed in the colonies was a financial one. It would take a large sum of money to purchase type and paper needed for such an undertaking. Adding to the overhead was the considerable amount of time that would have to be invested in the project to set up the type.

This left the colonies in an impasse: they could not easily secure Bibles from abroad, and no one in the colonies was printing Bibles. Obviously this had an impact upon the economy of the colonies, especially in the book-selling sector. Yet it had a much greater impact upon the morality of the colonies, for the Bible—as even the founders recognized—was the unfailing antidote to immorality.

Robert Aitken
Source: Emmet Collection of Manuscripts Etc. Relating to American History. / The republican court. / Volume 1.

Congress and the Bible - A Historical Perspective

In the summer of 1777, three Presbyterian ministers, keenly realizing the necessity of a fresh supply of Bibles, petitioned the Continental Congress to arrange for a domestic printing of the Bible.[clxxiii]

> To the honorable Continental Congress of the United States of North America now sitting in Philadelphia.
>
> Honoured Gentlemen
>
> We the Ministers of the Gospel of Christ in the City of Philadelphia, whose names are under written, taking it into our serious consideration that in our present circumstances, books in general, and in particular, the holy Scriptures contained in the old and new Testaments are growing so scarce and dear, that we greatly fear that unless timely care be used to prevent it, we shall not have Bibles for our schools and families, and for the publick worship of God in our churches.
>
> We therefore think it our duty to our country and to the churches of Christ to lay this danger before this honourable house, humbly requesting that under your care, and by your encouragement, a copy of the holy Bible may be printed, so as to be sold nearly as cheap as the common Bibles, formerly imported from Britain and Ireland, were sold.

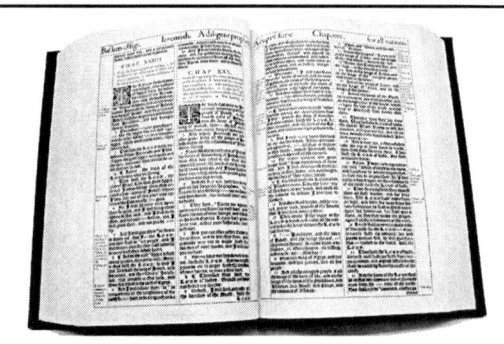

1611 First Edition King James Bible Facsimile Reproduction
Image courtesy of Gracious Christian Living, Inc.

The 1611 King James Bible
An original First Edition King James Bible measured 17" tall by 13" wide by 5" thick and weighed over 30 pounds. It was used primarily as a pulpit Bible.

In 1782 the King James Bible printed by Robert Aitken measured only 7.25" tall by 4.75" wide by 2.5" thick. It was intended for personal use.

> The number of purchasers is so great, that we doubt not but a large impression would soon be sold, But unless the sale of the whole edition belong to the printer, and he be bound under sufficient penalties, that no copy be sold by him, nor by any retailer under him, at a higher price than allowed by this honourable house, we fear that the whole impression would soon be bought up, and sold again at an exorbitant price, which would frustrate your pious endeavours and fill the country with just complaints.
>
> We are persuaded that your care and seasonable interposition will remove the anxious fears of many pious and well disposed persons; would prevent the murmurs of the discontented; would save much money to the United States; would be the means of promoting Christian knowledge in our churches, and would transmit your names with additional honour to the latest posterity.
>
> Our sincere prayers shall ever be for your welfare and prosperity, and we beg leave with the greatest respect to subscribe our selves.
>
> Honoured Gentlemen
> Your most obedient humble servants
> Francis Alison, John Ewing, William Marshalle[clxxiv]

This petition was referred to a committee composed of John Adams, Daniel Roberdeau, and Jonathan Bayard Smith. On September 11, 1777 the committee gave the following report:

> The committee appointed to consider the memorial of the Rev. Dr. Allison and others, report, "That they have conferred fully with the printers, &c. in this city, and are of the opinion, that the proper types for printing the Bible are not to be had in this country, and that the paper cannot be procured, but with such difficulties and subject to such casualties, as render any dependence on it altogether improper: that to import types for the purpose of setting up an entire edition of the Bible, and to strike off 30,000 copies, with paper, binding &c. will cost £10,272 10, which must be advanced by Congress, to be reimbursed by the sale of the books:

> **Historical Note:**
>
> In September of 1777, the Continental Congress was forced to abandon Philadelphia as the British attacked the city. The city was captured on September 26, 1777, and Congress never implemented any of the recommendations of the committee's report. The British garrisoned 9,000 troops in Germantown, five miles to the north.
>
> ***Germantown Battle, Chew's house***
> by Rawdon, Wright, and Harch from drawing by
> Koeltner ca. 1924.
> Public Domain.

"That, your committee are of opinion, considerable difficulties will attend the procuring the types and paper; that, afterwards, the risque of importing them will considerably enhance the cost, and that the calculations are that Congress cannot much rely on them: that the use of the Bible is so universal, and its importance so great, that your committee refer the above to the consideration of Congress, and if Congress shall not think it expedient to order the importation of types and paper, your committee recommend that Congress will order the Committee of Commerce to import 20,000 Bibles from Holland, Scotland, or elsewhere, into the different ports of the states in the Union."[clxxv]

Second Battle of the Virginia Capes
by V. Zveg, ca. 1962.
Public Domain.

The battle was strategically a major defeat for the British, since it prevented the Royal Navy from reinforcing or evacuating the blockaded forces. Throughout the war the Royal Navy blockaded colonial ports interferring with commerce and military supplies.

The committee's report was then put to vote, with seven colonies voting for it and six voting against it. Although the report had passed, probably because Congress was so evenly divided, it was ordered that "the consideration be postponed to Saturday next, to be taken up after reading the public letters."[clxxvi] However, possibly due to pressing matters connected with the ongoing war, Congress never implemented any of the recommendations of the committee's report.[clxxvii]

On October 26, 1780, the issue of Bible supply was again brought to the attention of Congress. At this time Congress passed the following resolution:

Resolved, That it be recommended to such of the States who may think it convenient for them that they take proper measures to procure one or more new and correct editions of the Old and New Testament to be printed and that such states regulate their printers by law so as to secure effectually the said books from being misprinted.[clxxviii]

Charles Thomson

Charles Thomson faithfully served as the secretary of the Continental Congress through its entirety. Over the course of those 15 years, the Congress saw many delegates come and go, but Thomson's dedication to recording the debates and decisions provided continuity. Along with John Hancock, president of the Congress, Thomson's name (as secretary) appeared on the first published version of the Declaration of Independence in July 1776.

Charles Thomson
by Joseph Wright, ca. 1783.
Public Domain.

Little more is known about this resolution except that it had been introduced by James McLene of Pennsylvania and seconded by John Hanson of Maryland.[clxxix] This resolution also seems to have had little results, as did the resolution of 1777.

Numerous scholars have speculated as to why Congress never acted upon the Bible committee's report of 1777. Derek H. Davis submits, quite convincingly, that while Congress was deeply committed to the importance of religion and the Bible, it was unwilling to become financially involved.[clxxx] Also, Congress was divided on this issue. Added to this dilemma was the fact that Congress was bankrupt: it did not have money on hand with which to purchase Bibles.

Since Congress was not actively pursuing Bible printing or importation, a Philadelphia printer, Robert Aitken (1734–1802), decided to begin printing his own Bibles. Aitken had moved from his native Scotland in 1769 and had begun selling "the very best books."[clxxxi] Having achieved success, he returned to Scotland in 1771 and brought his wife and two children to Philadelphia to be with him. He then located nearly opposite the London Coffee House. Here he began to print newspapers and books and soon operated the largest and best stocked bookstore in Philadelphia. Around this time, Aitken also became the official printer for Congress, printing the *Congressional Journal*.

The Old London Coffee House
The Library Company of Philadelphia

The Second London Coffee House, opened in 1754 by William Bradford, the Printer

It was a place of commercial and political conversation and debate. Up until the Revolutionary War, when it was closed by the British, it was the most popular Tavern in Philadelphia.

At the London Coffee House, Aitken rubbed shoulders with the Signers of the Declaration of Independence.[clxxxii] Through personal encounters and through his role as Congress's official printer, Aitken would have surely become aware of Congress's desire to see a Bible accurately printed in the colonies. And he possessed the credentials to undertake such a project. After all, he had a reputation for business acumen and was known for his accuracy. Possibly he received encouragement from members of Congress to pursue the printing of the Bible. He did receive approval for a loan of £150 from the General Assembly of the Commonwealth of Pennsylvania.[clccciii] (This was actually quite a small amount, since Congress had estimated that the printing of 30,000 Bibles would cost more than £10,000.) Now, Aitken was ready to secure funds and a recommendation from Congress for his enterprise.

On January 21, 1781, Robert Aitken presented a memorial to Congress.

> To the Honourable The Congress
> Of the United States of America
> The Memorial of Robert Aitken
> of the City of Philadelphia, Printer
>
> Humbly Sheweth
>
> That in every well regulated Government in Chistendom The Sacred Books of the Old and New Testament, commonly called the Holy Bible, are printed and published under the Authority of the Sovereign Powers, in order to prevent the fatal confusion that would arise and the alarming Injuries the Christian Faith might suffer from the Spurious and erroneous Editions of Divine Revelation. That your Memorialist has no doubt but this work is an Object worthy the attention of the Congress of the United States of America, who will not neglect spiritual security, while they are virtuously contending for temporal blessings.

> Under this persuasion your Memorialist begs leave to inform your Honours That he both begun and made considerable progress in a neat Edition of the Holy Scriptures for the use of schools, But being cautious of suffering his copy of the Bible to Issue forth without the sanction of Congress, Humbly prays that your Honours would take this important matter into serious consideration & would be pleased to appoint one Member or Members of your Honourable Body to inspect his work so that the same may be published under the Authority of Congress. And further, your Memorialist prays, that he may be commissioned or otherwise appointed & Authorized to print and vend Editions of the Sacred Scriptures, in such manner and form as may best suit the wants and demands of the good people of these States, provided the same be in all things perfectly consonant to the Scriptures as heretofore Established and received amongst us.[clxxxiv]

Entered into the Journals of the Continental Congress on January 26, 1781 was this brief statement:

> A memorial of Robert Aitkin was read:
> Ordered, That it be referred to the committee on the motion for printing the old and new Testament.[clxxxv]

On September 1, 1782, having heard that Aitken was almost finished with his Bible, the "committee on the motion for printing the old and new Testament" appointed the chaplains of Congress—the Rev. Dr. William White and the Rev. Mr. George Duffield—to examine the new edition for accuracy.

Before the chaplains completed their examination, Aitken sent another memorial to Congress. It was dated September 9 and informed Congress that his Bible "accomplished in the midst of the Confusion and Distresses of War" was completed.[clxxxvi] In this second memorial, Robert Aitken requested that Congress would purchase a fourth of the printing,—a request that was never granted.

On September 10, 1782, the chaplains submitted their report to "the committee on the motion for printing the old and new Testament." The committee accepted their approval and prepared a resolution authorizing Robert Aitken to print his Bible. On September 12, said committee presented their resolution and recommendation to Congress. The following was entered into the Journals of the Continental Congress:

The committee, consisting of Mr. [James] Duane, Mr. [Thomas] McKean and Mr. [John] Witherspoon, to whom was referred a memorial of Robert Aitken, printer, dated 21 January, 1781, respecting an edition of the holy scriptures, report,

That Mr. Aitken has at a great expence now finished an American edition of the holy scriptures in English; that the committee have, from time to time, attended to his progress in the work: that they also recommended it to the two chaplains of Congress to examine and give their opinion of the execution, who have accordingly reported thereon:

The recommendation and report being as follows:

Philadelphia, 1 September, 1782.

Rev. Gentlemen, Our knowledge of your piety and public spirit leads us without apology to recommend to your particular attention the edition of the holy scriptures publishing by Mr. Aitken. He undertook this expensive work at a time, when from the circumstances of the war, an English edition of the Bible could not be imported, nor any opinion formed how long the obstruction might continue. On this account particularly he deserves applause and encouragement. We therefore wish you, revered gentlemen, to examine the execution of the work, and if approved, to give it the sanction of your judgment and the weight of your recommendation. We are with very great respect, your most obedient humble servants,

(Signed) James Duane, Chairman,
In behalf of a committee of Congress on Mr. Aitken's memorial.
Rev. Dr. White and Rev. Mr. Duffield, chaplains of
the United States in Congress assembled.

Report

Gentlemen, Agreeably to your desire, we have paid attention to Mr. Robert Aitken's impression of the holy scriptures, of the old and new testament. Having selected and examined a variety of passages throughout the work, we are of opinion, that it is executed with great accuracy as to the sense, and with as few grammatical and typographical errors as could be expected in an undertaking of such magnitude. Being ourselves witnesses of the demand for this invaluable book, we rejoice in the present prospect of a supply, hoping that it will prove advantageous as it is honorable to the gentleman, who has exerted himself to furnish it at the evident risk of private fortune. We are, gentlemen, your very respectful and humble servants,

(Signed) William White,
George Duffield.

Philadelphia, September 10, 1782.
Hon. James Duane, esq. chairman,
and the other hon. Gentlemen of the committee of Congress on Mr. Aitken's memorial.

Whereupon, Resolved, That the United States in Congress assembled, highly approve the pious and laudable undertaking of Mr. Aitken, as subservient to the interest of religion as well as an instance of the progress of arts in this country, and being satisfied from the above report, of his care and accuracy in the execution of the work, they recommend this edition of the Bible to the inhabitants of the United States, and hereby authorise him to publish this recommendation in the manner he shall think proper.[clxxxvii]

> BY THE UNITED STATES IN CONGRESS ASSEMBLED:
>
> September 12th, 1782.
>
> THE Committee to whom was referred a Memorial of Robert Aitken, Printer, dated 21st January, 1781, respecting an edition of the Holy Scriptures, report, "That Mr. Aitken has, at a great expence, now finished an American edition of the Holy Scriptures in English; that the Committee have from time to time attended to his progress in the work; that they also recommended it to the two Chaplains of Congress to examine and give their opinion of the execution, who have accordingly reported thereon; the recommendation and report being as follows:
>
> "Philadelphia, 1st September, 1782."

> Honble James Duane, Esq. Chairman, and the other Honble Gentlemen of the Committee of Congress on Mr. Aitken's Memorial."
>
> Whereupon,
> RESOLVED,
> THAT the United States in Congress assembled highly approve the pious and laudable undertaking of Mr. Aitken, as subservient to the interest of religion, as well as an instance of the progress of arts in this country, and being satisfied from the above report of his care and accuracy in the execution of the work, they recommend this edition of the Bible to the inhabitants of the United States, and hereby authorise him to publish this Recommendation in the manner he shall think proper.
>
> CHA. THOMSON, Sec'ry.

Journals of the Continental Congress

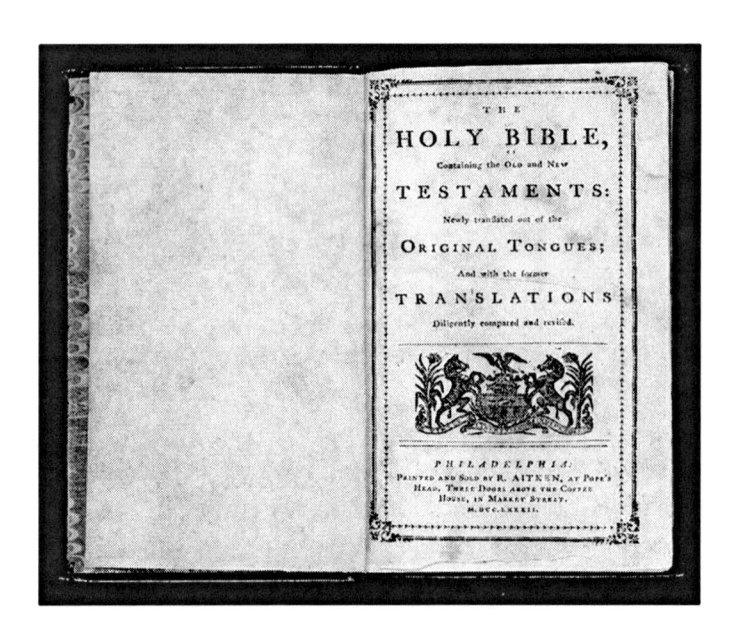

Original 1782 Aitken Bible
Library of Congress

When Aitken's Bible was issued on September 25, he sent a complimentary copy to John Hanson, president of the Continental Congress. In the opening pages, Aitken had printed the four endorsements received from Congress. Also, on the same day, he placed an advertisement for his Bible in the *Freeman's Journal*.

Robert Aitken's Bible was bound both in one and two-volume editions. For the most part, the volumes measured five and one-half inches by three and one-eighth inches. And, because of the exorbitant price of paper, the margins were quite small. Further, Aitken printed around 10,000 copies of the Bible. And since Congress provided no funding for this project, he turned to another method of sales: he sold copies to other printers and store owners who would, in turn, sell the Bibles; he also bought advertising and sold Bibles directly to the public. However, his timing was a bit tardy, for the war was nearing an end. When it did end, international trade resumed, bringing less expensive and better quality Bibles to the American market. This, obviously, was economically devastating to Robert Aitken.

To offset his losses, a friend of Aitken's—Dr. John Rodgers, pastor of the First Presbyterian Church in New York—wrote to General George Washington, requesting that copies of Aitken's Bible be purchased and presented to each of the soldiers under his command. Washington replied that the request had come too late, as two thirds of the army had already been discharged. Washington's reply, dated June 11, 1783, read:

> Dear Sir,
>
> I accept with much pleasure you kind Congratulations on the happy Event of Peace, with the establishment of our Liberties & Independence.
>
> Glorious indeed has been our Contest:—glorious, if we consider the prize for which we have contended, and glorious in its Issue:—But in the mist of our Joys, I hope we shall not forget that, to Divine Providence is to be ascribed the Glory & the Praise.

Your Proposition respecting Mr. Aitken's Bible would have been particularly noticed by me, had it been suggested in season. But the late Resolution of Congress for discharging Part of the Army, taking off near two thirds of our Numbers, it is now too late to make the Attempt. It would have pleased me well, if Congress had been pleased to make such an important present to the brave fellows, who have done so much for the Security of their Country's rights & Establishment.

I hope it will not be long before you will be able to go quietly to N. York—some Patience however will yet be necessary. But Patience is a noble virtue, and when rightly exercised, does not fail of its reward.

With much Regard & Esteem
I am Dear Doctor
Your most obed. Servant
G. Washington[clxxxviii]

George Washington Resigns His Commission
by John Trumbull, ca. 1824.
Public Domain.

Aitken did receive a limited amount of help from the Philadelphia Synod of the Presbyterian Church, which purchased some of his Bibles to distribute among the poor. However, this was not enough to keep the Philadelphia printer from financial ruin.

Nevertheless, Robert Aitken continued in the printing business, producing fine specimens of that trade. In an effort to recoup his losses, in 1789 he petitioned Congress for a patent to hold exclusive rights to print Bibles for 14 years—a petition that was denied. These losses were at the forefront of his mind when, two years later, Aitken wrote to John Nicholson, receiver of general taxes for the Commonwealth of Pennsylvania:

> I have calculated from my true loss by Continental money 3,000 and on the Edition of 10,000 Bibles 4,000—owing to these you may readily figure my situation. My house is under mortgage for a considerable sum, a foreign debt, though not of its value. I have other debts to pay, not considerable—what I earn goes to pay them as soon as earned.[clxxxix]

Robert Aitken ended life as a debtor; however, he passed on a noble trade and stellar qualities. Concerning the passing on of his trade, Aitken's daughter Jane became a printer and book binder. In fact, it was she who printed Charles Thomson's English translation of the Greek Septuagint Old Testament, the first translation of the Septuagint into English. It should be remembered that Charles Thomson was the secretary of the Continental Congress throughout its duration.

When Robert Aitken died in 1802, the *Gazette of the United States* printed the following in its July 2 edition:

> On the 14th in the 68th year of his age, Mr. Robert Aitken Sen. Of this city, Printer: near 40 years a respectable inhabitant of this city; through the whole of an useful life regarded for his integrity and probity; and leaving behind him a family, carefully brought up in the paths of industry and virtue.[cxc]

What a fitting eulogy for the man who risked personal wealth to print the Scriptures.

Today, less than 30 copies of the Aitken Bible are known to exist.[cxci] Two are known to be listed for sale, with an individual asking price of $145,000.

Summary

In more recent times, a debate has existed over what Congress endorsed in respect to Robert Aitken's Bible. Did Congress merely endorse the accuracy of the Bible, or did it endorse the accuracy and the undertaking of the Bible? I submit that it was the latter. For starters, look at Congress' resolution:

> Whereupon, Resolved, That the United States in Congress assembled, highly approve the pious and laudable undertaking of Mr. Aitken, as subservient to the interest of religion as well as an instance of the progress of arts in this country, and being satisfied from the above report, of his care and accuracy in the execution of the work, they recommend this edition of the Bible to the inhabitants of the United States, and hereby authorise him to publish this recommendation in the manner he shall think proper.[cxcii]

Notice that the resolution does the following:

(1) It approved the pious and laudable "undertaking" of Mr. Aitken. The word undertaking takes in the full scope of the project, not simply the limited aspect of accuracy.

(2) It recognized that the printing of the Bible was vital to the interest of religion.

(3) It acknowledged that the printing of the Bible promoted the progress of arts. After all, Aitken's Bible was the first English Bible printed in North America.

(4) It allowed that Aitken's Bible was accurate.

(5) It authorized Aitken to utilize Congress' recommendation in any manner he thought proper. Congress was privy to the fact that Aitken needed a way to sell Bibles, and its allowance that Aitken use its recommendation would certainly be helpful to Aitken for advertising purposes.

By seriously considering the aforementioned Congressional resolution, it becomes quite obvious that Congress endorsed the Aitken Bible as worthy of purchase by American citizenry. Those who submit that Congress' resolution was simply recognition of the Aitken Bible's accuracy fail to factor in the language of the resolution, language which includes words such as "approve", "laudable undertaking", "recommend", and "authorize".

Another debate centers on why Congress endorsed the Aitken Bible. On one side are those who posit that Congress was interested in the religious well-being of the colonies, saw the need of Bibles within the colonies, and appreciated the undertaking of Mr. Aitken. On the other side are those who postulate that Congress was simply interested in being kind to Aitken. This position was advanced by Edwin Rumball-Petre in 1940. He wrote that as the printer of the Journals of Congress, Aitken was a friend of Congress, and, when it appeared as if Aitken would suffer personal financial loss, Congress came to his aid. While this friendship aspect may be a part to the puzzle, I believe it to be only a small part.

One final question may be stated thus: "Why did Congress not underwrite the printing of the Aitken Bible?" Derek H. Davis responds:

> Laboring without the restraints on its involvement in religion that would follow the passage of the Constitution's First Amendment, Congress probably did not perceive the project as an improper advancement of religion. It did, however, seem to view as one of its primary responsibilities the preservation of the liberty of the various states in things pertaining to religion. Therefore, it is more likely that congress believed that because of the likelihood that the Aitken Bible would not appeal to all citizens of the various states, it would be an infringement upon the states' liberty for Congress, which represented all of the states, to expend the monies required to publish the needed Bibles.[cxciii]

CHAPTER SIX

THE BIBLE AND U.S. CONGRESS

Shortly after the Capitol building in Washington, D.C. was completed in 1800, Congress approved its use for church services. By 1867, the church at the Capitol was the largest in the city, with attendance as high as 2,000 a week. Thomas Jefferson attended these Capitol services, and even had the Marine Band play. Notably, the Bible was a prominent part of these Capitol services. It was not seen as breaking down any church and state barriers. Instead it was welcomed.

Washington Capitol, 1800
Public Domain.

Concerning the role the Bible served in the United States, Robert Winthrop, who served as the Speaker of the House of Representatives (1847–1849), ably stated:

> The voice of experience and the voice of our own reason speak but one language. . . . Both united in teaching us that men may as well build their houses upon the sand and expect to see them stand, when the rains fall, and the winds blow, and the floods come, as to found free institutions upon

any other basis that that of morality and virtue, of which the Word of God is the only authoritative rule, and the only adequate sanction.

All societies of men must be governed in some way or other. The less they have of stringent state government, the more they must have of individual self-government. The less they rely on public law or physical force, the more they must rely on private moral restraint.

Men, in a word, must necessarily be controlled either by a power within them or a power without them; either by the Word of God or by the strong arm of man; either by the Bible or by the bayonet.

It may do for other countries and other governments to talk about the state supporting religion. Here, under our own free institutions, it is religion which must support the state.[cxciv]

In 1852, Daniel Webster, a former U.S. congressman and senator, delivered a speech before the Historical Society of New York in which he declared:

If we and our posterity shall be true to the Christian religion, if we and they shall live always in the fear of God, and shall respect His commandments, if we and they shall maintain just moral sentiments and such conscientious convictions of duty as shall control the heart and life, we may have the highest hopes of the future fortunes of our country; and if we maintain those institutions of government and that political union, exceeding all praise as much as it exceeds all former examples of political associations, we may be sure of one thing, that while our country furnishes material for a thousand masters of the historic art, it will afford prospering and to prosper. But if we and our posterity reject religious institutions and authority, violate the rules no topic for a Gibbon.

It will have no decline and fall. It will go on of eternal justice, trifle with the injunctions of morality, and recklessly destroy the political constitution which holds us together, no man can tell how sudden a catastrophe may overwhelm us that shall bury all our glory in profound obscurity.[cxcv]

At this juncture of our history, America still retained somewhat of a biblical foundation. This led James Bryce of England to comment in 1888 that in America "there are churches everywhere and everywhere equally... Possibly half of the native population go to church at least once every Sunday."[cxcvi]

Portrait of Daniel Webster by Francis Alexander ca. 1835. Public Domain.

He also commented that the reading of the average family had a "religious tinge," for most families read religious books and magazines.[cxcvii] Bryce's sentiments were echoed by Czechoslovakian Francis Grund two years later. "The religious habits of Americans form not only the basis of their private and public morals but have become ... thoroughly interwoven with ... the very essence of their government."[cxcviii] He commented further that religion "presides over their councils, aids in the execution of the laws, and adds to the dignity of the judges."[cxcix]

Yet for all this religiosity, America began to forsake the Bible. Shortly after World War I (1914–1918), the United States entered into a transitional period. This transition had begun "almost imperceptibly, in the late 1870s and 1880s."[cc]

Webster's Reply to Hayne
by George P. A. Healy, ca. 1830.
Public Domain.

Theology professors at American seminaries began to interject German criticism and religious liberalism into their courses. At the heart of this criticism was the questioning of the Bible's authority. In addition, human reason was elevated. All this resulted in pastors graduating from the seminaries and preaching their criticism-laden sermons to the populace. The net result was men and women across the nation doubting the authority of Scripture. Numbers even abandoned the Bible. After all, why believe in a book that is chock-full of mistakes and no longer authoritative?

Around this same time, America entered into a decade of prosperity and frivolity called the "Roaring Twenties." Much of this economic boast was due to assembly-line production, mass consumption, easy credit, and advertising. Wealth was widespread and families—although not all—began to indulge in entertainment and leisure. In the process, large swaths of America forgot God and the Bible (Deuteronomy 8:14). As a result, moral decay began to eat away at the warp and woof of the nation's fiber.

Because Congress is elected by the people, and because the American people were fast becoming biblically illiterate and insensitive, Congress as a body no longer evidenced a familiarity with the Book of all Books. Yes, the Bible was still quoted and alluded to, but not like before. However, Congress did, from time to time, still involve itself with the Bible.

For example, in 1931 Congress adopted the "Star-Spangled Banner" as the official National anthem. The "Star-Spangled Banner" contains phrases such as "May the Heav'n-rescued land Praise the Power that hath made and preserved us a nation" and "This be our motto, 'In God is our trust!'" Next, Congress added the phrase "one nation under God" to the Pledge of Allegiance in 1954. Also, in 1954, Congress added a Congressional Prayer Room with a stained glass window bearing the likeness of George Washington kneeling in prayer. On this window is Psalm 16:1: "Preserve me, O God, for in Thee do I put my trust."

In 1983, "The Congress of the United States, in recognition of the unique contribution of the Bible in shaping the history and character of this nation and so many of its citizens" requested President Ronald Reagan to designate the year 1983 as the "Year of the Bible."[cci] The Proclamation read:

Proclamation 5018—Year of the Bible, 1983
February 3, 1983
By the President of the United States of America

A Proclamation

Of the many influences that have shaped the United States of America into a distinctive Nation and people, none may be said to be more fundamental and enduring than the Bible.

Deep religious beliefs stemming from the Old and New Testaments of the Bible inspired many of the early settlers of our country, providing them with the strength, character, convictions, and faith necessary to withstand great hardship and danger in this new and rugged land.

These shared beliefs helped forge a sense of common purpose among the widely dispersed colonies—a sense of community which laid the foundation for the spirit of nationhood that was to develop in later decades.

The Bible and its teachings helped form the basis for the Founding Fathers' abiding belief in the inalienable rights of the individual, rights which they found implicit in the Bible's teachings of the inherent worth and dignity of each individual. This same sense of man patterned the convictions of those who framed the English system of law inherited by our own Nation, as well as the ideals set forth in the Declaration of Independence and the Constitution.

For centuries the Bible's emphasis on compassion and love for our neighbor has inspired institutional and governmental expressions of benevolent outreach such as private charity, the establishment of schools and hospitals, and the abolition of slavery.

Many of our greatest national leaders—among them Presidents Washington, Jackson, Lincoln, and Wilson—have recognized the influence of the Bible on our country's development. The plainspoken Andrew Jackson referred to the Bible as no less than "the rock on which our Republic rests." Today our beloved America and, indeed, the world, is facing a decade of enormous challenge. As a people we may well be tested as we have seldom, if ever, been tested before. We will need resources of spirit even more than resources of technology, education, and armaments. There could be no more fitting moment than now to reflect with gratitude, humility, and urgency upon the wisdom revealed to us in the writing that Abraham Lincoln called "the best gift God has ever given to man . . . But for it we could not know right from wrong."

The Congress of the United States, in recognition of the unique contribution of the Bible in shaping the history and character of this Nation, and so many of its citizens, has by Senate Joint Resolution 165 authorized and requested the President to designate the year 1983 as the "Year of the Bible."

Now, Therefore, I, Ronald Reagan, President of the United States of America, in recognition of the contributions and influence of the Bible on our Republic and our people, do hereby proclaim 1983 the Year of the Bible in the United States. I encourage all citizens, each in his or her own way, to reexamine and rediscover its priceless and timeless message.

In Witness Whereof, I have hereunto set my hand this third day of February, in the year of our Lord nineteen hundred and eighty-three, and of the Independence of the United States of America the two hundred and seventh.

Ronald Reagan[ccii]

Portrait of Ronald Reagan
by Everett Raymond Kinstler,
ca. 1991.
Public Domain.

In the last seven years, at least 10 resolutions have been introduced into the House and/or Senate that have in some manner dealt with the Bible. Not one has passed.

1. H. Con. Res. 12 (Introduced January 3, 2005, 109th Congress)
• Requiring the display of the Ten Commandments in the Hall of the House of Representatives and the Chamber of the Senate

2. H. Con. Res. 12 (Introduced January 3, 2005, 109th Congress)
• Requiring the display of the Ten Commandments in the United States Capitol

3. H. Res. 214 (Introduced April 13, 2005, 109th Congress)
• Directing the Speaker of the House of Representatives to provide for the display of the Ten Commandments in the chamber of the House of Representatives

4. H. Con. Res. 194 (July 27, 2005, 109th Congress)
• Expressing the sense of the Congress that the display of the Ten Commandments in public buildings does not violate the First Amendment to the constitution of the United States

5. H. J. Res. 57 (Introduced August 22, 2005, 109th Congress)
• Proposing an amendment to the Constitution of the United States protecting religious freedom

6. H. Con. Res. 431 (Introduced June 20, 2006, 109th Congress)
• Calling on the President to proclaim 2007 as the "National Year of the Bible"

7. H. Con. Res. 12 (Introduced January 4, 2007, 110th Congress)
• Requiring the display of the Ten Commandments in the United States Capitol

8. H. Con. Res. 284 (Introduced January 28, 2008, 110th Congress)
• Encouraging the President to proclaim 2008 as "The National Year of the Bible"

9. S. Res. 483 (Introduced March 12, 2008, 110th Congress)
• A resolution recognizing the first weekend of May 2008 as "Ten Commandments Weekend"

10. H. Con. Res. 38 (Introduced April 12, 2011, 112th Congress)
• Recognizing the 400th anniversary of the publication of the King James Version of the Bible.

Summary

While brave-hearted senators and representatives still exist (for they have sponsored and co-sponsored the aforementioned resolutions), Congress as a whole has largely abandoned the Bible. And while the Bible is still ceremonially utilized at inaugurations, it is pragmatically denied a place in government. For example: "three plaques, with verses from Psalms on them posted at lookouts over the Grand Canyon, were removed by the Department of Interior following threats by the ACLU, which claimed the verses were an illegal endorsement of religion by the government."[cciii]

"A U.S. District Court judge ordered the removal of a Bible from a monument that sat in front of the Harris County courthouse in Houston Texas for 50 years, on the grounds that it violated separation of church and state."[cciv]

"The Colorado Supreme Court commuted the death penalty conviction of a man on death row (who had kidnapped, raped, and murdered a woman) on the grounds that one of the jurors used the Bible in the decision-making process."[cv]

"The highest judicial figure in the state of Alabama was expelled from the court for his refusal to remove a Ten Commandments monument from the foyer of the judiciary."[ccvi]

EPILOGUE:

WHAT ROLE SHOULD THE BIBLE HAVE IN AMERICA TODAY?

The answer to the question, "What role should the Bible have in America Today?," is quite simple. It should serve the same role and occupy the same position it did during America's founding. And Congress has a vital responsibility in this area. It can help determine whether the Bible is promoted or demoted, whether it is championed or condemned.

If Congress wants to promote and champion the Bible, it can do so, just like the Founders. For example, it can still quote the Bible in official documents. Its members can include the Bible in their speeches. It can continue to chisel Bible verses into the marble and granite of national monuments and the walls of U.S. government buildings. It can promote the printing of Bibles. It can base its laws upon the Bible's precepts and principles. It can pass laws giving the Bible a place in our courts, schools, and public spaces. Most important, its members can and should embrace the Bible personally.

Yet, by and large, this is not happening. Instead, the Bible is systematically being removed from its prominence in our nation.

The First Amendment

In 1789 Congress approved the First Amendment to the U.S. Constitution which read:

> Congress shall make no law respecting an establishment of religion, or prohibiting the free exercise thereof; or abridging the freedom of speech, or of the press, or the right of the people peaceably to assemble, and to petition the Government for a redress of grievances.

This amendment prohibited Congress from establishing an official state church or religion. In addition, this amendment kept Congress from making laws that even dealt with the issue of establishing an official state church or religion—this legal territory was reserved for the states.

However, Congress did not interpret the First Amendment to mean that it could not involve itself with religion in general. This is proven by simply noting the actions of Congress the day after it adopted the First Amendment. On that day Congress passed a resolution stating:

> Resolved, that a joint committee of both Houses be directed to wait upon the President of the United States, to request that he would recommend to the people of the United States a day of public thanksgiving and prayer, to be observed by acknowledging, with grateful hearts, the many signal favors of Almighty God, especially by affording them an opportunity peaceable to establish a Constitution of government for their safety and happiness.[ccvii]

President George Washington complied with Congress's resolution, and on November 26, 1789, urged all Americans to "unite in most humbly offering our prayers and supplications to the great Lord and ruler of Nations, and beseech him to pardon our national and other transgressions."[ccviii]

The resolution of Congress pertaining to the day of public thanksgiving and prayer did receive some opposition within Congress. Representative Thomas Tucker of South Carolina argued that a day of public thanksgiving and prayer "is a business with which Congress [should] have nothing to do; it is a religious matter, and, as such, is proscribed to us."[ccix] However, the majority of Tucker's colleagues did not agree: they believed that setting a day of public thanksgiving and prayer to be within their realm of jurisdiction. They also believed it to be their prerogative to enact a law providing for the compensation of congressional chaplains, a law passed two days before the House of Representatives approved the final wording of the First Amendment.

Joseph Story, a U.S. Supreme Court justice from 1811–1845 stated concerning the First Amendment:

> Probably at the time of the adoption of the Constitution, and of the amendment to it now under consideration, the general if not the universal sentiment in America was that Christianity ought to receive encouragement from the State so far as was not incompatible with the private rights of conscience and the freedom of religious worship. An attempt to level all religions, and to make it a matter of state policy to hold all in utter indifference, would have created universal disapprobation, if not universal indignation.[ccx]

Story went on later to state:

> The real object of the First Amendment was not to countenance, much less to advance, Mahametanism, or Judaism, or infidelity, by prostrating Christianity; but to exclude all rivalry among Christian sects, and to prevent any national ecclesiastical establishment which should give to a hierarchy the exclusive patronage of the national government. It thus cut off the means of religious persecution (the vice and pest of former ages), and of the subversion of the rights of conscience in matters of religion which had been trampled upon almost from the days of the Apostles to the present age . . .[ccxi]

Throughout most of its history, America and its Congress have operated with the premise that religion was welcome in government. In fact every president from George Washington to Barack Obama has been sworn in to office on the Bible, stating at the end, "So help me God." Nearly every president has also acknowledged God in his inaugural address.

Nevertheless, a major shift occurred in 1947. This is when the U.S. Supreme Court heard the case Everson v. Board of Education; its majority decision, in part, declared:

> Neither a state nor a Federal Government can, openly or secretly, participate in the affairs of any religious organizations or groups and vice versa. In the words of Jefferson, the clause against establishment of religion by law was intended to erect "a wall of separation between Church and State."[ccxii]

For starters, Jefferson—who coined the phrase "a wall of separation between Church and State" in a personal letter—was taken out of context by the high court. Jefferson believed the "wall" to be between the federal government and established religion. To this end, Jefferson wrote to the Rev. Samuel Miller:

> I consider the government of the United States as interdicted by the Constitution from inter-meddling with religious institutions, their doctrines, discipline, or exercise. This results not only from the provision that no law shall be made respecting the establishment or free exercise of religion but from that also which reserves to the States the powers not delegated to the United States. Certainly no power to prescribe any religious exercise, or to assume authority in religious discipline, has been delegated to the General Government. It must then rest with the states, as far as it can be in any human authority.[ccxiii]

Obviously, Jefferson did not believe that the federal government could not be involved in religion, otherwise he would not have recommended to Congress the passage of a treaty providing $100 annually to support a Catholic priest who ministered to the Kaskaskia Indians.[ccxiv] Otherwise, Jefferson would not have signed into law "An Act regulating the grants of land appropriated for Military services and for the Society of the United Brethren for propagating the Gospel among the Heathen." Otherwise, Jefferson would have not permitted church services to be held in the U.S. Capitol building. Otherwise, Jefferson would not have attended a church service in the Capitol building two days after he penned the words "a wall of separation between Church and State." Otherwise, Jefferson would not have ordered the Marine Band to play for the church services held in the Capitol.

The account is given regarding a conversation Jefferson had with the Rev. Ethan Allan while walking to church on Sunday (at the Capitol).

"Which way are you walking, Mr. Jefferson? Allen asked.

"To Church, Sir."

"You, Going to Church, Mr. J? You do not believe a word in it!"

"Sir," said Mr. Jefferson, "no nation has ever yet existed or been governed without religion. Nor can be. The Christian religion is the best religion that has been given to man and I as chief Magistrate of this nation am bound to give it the sanction of my example. Good morning, Sir."[ccxv]

Not only did the Everson v. Board of Education decision misinterpret Thomas Jefferson, it was also inconsistent with precedent. After all, the Bible and God are pictured all over Washington, D.C. For example, Moses is engraved near the top of the east (back) entrance of the U.S. Supreme Court building, holding tablets that have come to symbolically represent the Ten Commandments. At the Library of Congress are statues of Moses and Paul, the Giant Bible of Mainz and the Gutenberg Bible, as well as Scriptures painted upon the walls. These Scriptures announce: "The light shineth in darkness, and the darkness comprehendeth it not" (John 1:5); "Wisdom is the principal thing; therefore, get wisdom and with all thy getting, get understanding" (Proverbs 4:7); "What doth the Lord require of thee, but to do justly, and to love mercy, and to walk humbly with thy God" (Micah 6:8); and "The heavens declare the Glory of God, and the firmament showeth His handiwork" (Psalm 19:1). Further, Memorial blocks at the Washington Monument declare "Holiness to the Lord" (Exodus 28:36); "Search the Scriptures" (John 5:39); and "The memory of the just is blessed" (Proverbs 10:7). Over at the Lincoln Memorial one can read John 19:9 carved into granite: "the judgments of the Lord are true and righteous altogether." Yet that is not all. Inlaid at the entrance to the National Archives is a bronze medallion of the Ten Commandments.

Goodbye, Religious Freedom

Despite the presence of biblical imagery and words across our nation's capital, and despite the Everson v. Board of Education "misapplication of law and history," the U.S. Supreme Court has built a legal foundation upon said decision.[cxvi] Following are some further decisions based upon Everson v. Board of Education:

> A verbal prayer offered in school is unconstitutional, even if it is both denominationally neutral and voluntarily participated in. Engel v. Vitale, 1962; Abington v. Schempp, 1963; Commissioner of Education v. School Committee of Leyden, 1971.
>
> Freedom of speech is guaranteed to students who speak at school assemblies where attendance is voluntary unless that speech includes a prayer. Stein v. Oshinky, 1965; Collins v. Chandler Unified School District, 1981.
>
> If a student prays over lunch, it is unconstitutional for him to pray aloud. Reed v. van Hoven, 1965.
>
> It is unconstitutional for a Board of Education to "reference" God or "Biblical instruction" in any of its official writings related to standards for operation of schools. State v. Whisner, 1976.
>
> It is unconstitutional for a classroom library to contain books that deal with Christianity or for a teacher to be seen with a personal copy of the Bible at school. Roberts v. Madigan, 1990.
>
> It is unconstitutional for the Ten Commandments to hang on the walls of a classroom even if they are purchased by private funds. Stone v. Graham, 1980. Ring v. Grand Forks Public School District, 1980; Lanner v. Wimmer, 1981.[ccxvii]

"One month after the tragic 1999 shootings at Columbine High School near Denver, Colorado, one of the parents whose daughter had been killed went to Washington, D.C. to testify before Congress. As part of his testimony, Darrell Scott, father of the slain Rachel Scott, expressed his feelings in poetry about the current direction of America. Darrell testified:

> Your laws ignore our deepest needs
> Your words are empty air
> You've stripped away our heritage
> You've outlawed simple prayer
> Now gunshots fill our classrooms and
> Precious children die.
> You seek for answers everywhere
> And ask the question "Why?"
> You regulate restrictive laws
> Through legislative creed
> And yet you fail to understand
> That God is what we need.[ccxvii]

What Have We Lost?

If you have carefully read this book, you will realize that in America we have lost the biblical principles upon which we were founded. Thus, the Bible is no longer welcome in the halls of Congress or in the halls of our public schools. The Ten Commandments are banished from the walls of schools and from our courtrooms. And prayer in public places is condemned. Yet, the Founders valued the Bible, built upon biblical principles, quoted the Bible in Congress, utilized the Bible for presidential inaugurations, prayed, and encouraged the nation to pray.

Today we possess only shreds of what our nation used to be and stand for. Now we are at a crossroads. Here we have two primary choices: (1) we can either obey the Bible or (2) continue to trample the Bible under our feet. We can return to the principles upon which our nation was founded, or continue our downward trajectory. To those who choose the first option, the route is clear. The Bible declares:

> If my people, which are called by my name, shall humble themselves, and pray, and seek my face, and turn from their wicked ways; then will I hear from heaven, and will forgive their sin, and will heal their land
> (2 Chronicles 7:14).

Herein lies the answer for America and Congress. Outside of the Bible, no answer exists.

Index of Photos and Images

Preface	*Second Continental Congress*	Historical Society of Pennsylvania
Page 1	*The Great Citie*	NPS, Jamestown Historic Site
Page 2	*The Landing of John Smith*	Library of Virginia
Page 3	*The Baptism of Pocahontas*	Arch. of the Capitol
Page 4	*King James I of England and VI of Scotland*	NPG, London
Page 6	*The Departure of the Pilgrim Fathers, 1620*	Private Collection
Page 7	*Signing of the Mayflower Compact*	Pilgrim Hall Museum, Plymouth, MA
Pgs 10-23	*Colonial Seals*	ClipArt ETC. Unv. of S. Florida
Page 11	*King Charles I*	Louvre, Paris, France
Page 14	*King Charles II*	NPG, London
Page 19	*The Thirteen Colonies at the End of the Colonial Period*	Cambridge Modern History Atlas, 1912
Page 21	*William Penn*	Unknown
Page 22	*The Birth of Pennsylvania 1680*	Private Collection
Page 25	*Stamp Act Stamp*	ClipArt ETC. Unv. of S. Florida
Page 26	*Portrait of Benjamin Franklin*	NPG, London
Page 27	*Thomas Jefferson, 1791*	Library of Congress
Page 28	*Carpenter's Hall, Philadelphia*	The Historical Society of Pennsylvania
Page 29	*First Prayer in Congress*	Library of Congress
Page 31	*John Adams, 2nd President of US*	United States Navy
Page 33	*Patrick Henry*	Library of Congress
Page 35	*Portrait of King George, III*	NPG, London
Page 36	*Writing the Declaration of Independence*	Library of Congress

Index of Photos and Images

Page 40	*The Declaration of Independence of the United States of America, July 4, 1776*	White House Historical Association
Page 41	*Surrender of Lord Cornwallis*	Library of Congress
Page 44	*Scene at the Signing of the Constitution of the United States*	United States House of Representatives
Page 45	*George Washington before the Battle of Trenton*	Yale University Art Gallery
Page 47	*Washington as Statesman at the Constitutional Convention*	Virginia Museum of Fine Arts
Page 49	*Franklin at the Constitutional Convention 1787*	The Historical Society of Pennsylvania
Page 50	*The March to Valley Forge*	The American Revolution Center
Page 55	*The Washington Family*	National Gallery of Art
Page 56	*The Declaration of Independence*	United States Capitol
Page 57	*A Popular History of the United States*	New York: Charles Scribners' Sons, 1881
Page 60	*Images from 1902 Facsimile of Jefferson Bible*	Smithsonian National Museum/Amrcn History
Page 61	*Portrait of John Jay*	National Gallery of Art
Page 64	*Engraving after a painting by Alonzo Chappel*	Philadelphia: Geroge W. Jacobs and Co., 1904
Page 65	*Boston Harbor*	Boston Public Library
Page 68	*Jonathan Edwards*	New Haven, CT: Durrie and Peck
	Sinners in the Hands of an Angry God	Rare Books Division, the New York Public Library

INDEX OF PHOTOS AND IMAGES

Page 71	*Portrait of George Washington*	Clark Art Instituite
	Portrait of Thomas Jefferson	White House Hist. Assc.
	Portrait of John Jay	National Portrait Gallery Smithsonian National Museum, WA DC
	Portrait of Samuel Adams	The life and public services of Samuel Adams
Page 73	*Portrait of Robert Aitken*	NY Public Library
Page 74	*KJB Facsimile*	Photo courtesy GCL
Page 76	*Germantown Battle, Chews House*	National Archives Records and Admin.
Page 77	*Second Battle of the Virginia Capes*	Hampton Roads Naval Museum, Norfolk, VA
Page 78	*Portrait of Charles Thomson*	Private Collector
Page 79	*The Old London Coffee House*	Library Company of Philadelphia
Page 84	*Journals of the Continetal Congress*	Library of Congress
	Original 1782 Aitken Bible	Library of Congress
Page 86	*G. Washington Resigns His Commission*	Capitol Rotunda
Page 89	*Washington Capitol, 1800*	Hesse-Wartegg's "Nord Amerika, 1800
Page 91	*Portrait of Daniel Webster*	Dartmouth College
Page 92	*Webster's Reply to Hayne*	NPS, Boston, MA
Page 95	*Portrait of Ronald Reagan*	National Portrait Gallery Smithsonian National Museum, WA DC

NOTES

[i] "The First English Language Bible Published in North America," <http://myloc.gov/Exhibitions/Bibles/OtherBibles/ExhibitObjects/TheFirstEnglishLanguageBiblePublishedinNorthAmerica.aspx> (accessed 23 May 2012).

[ii] Donald S. Lutz, "The Relative Influence of European Writers on Late Eighteenth Century American Political Thought," American Political Science Review 78 (1984), 189–197.

[iii] James H. Hutson, *Religion and the Founding of the American Republic* (Washington, D.C.: Library of Congress, 1998), 3.

[iv] Richard Hildreth, *The History of the United States of America: From the Discovery of the Continent to the Organization of Government under the Federal Constitution*, 1497–1789, Vol. 1 (New York: Harper and Brothers, 1854), 96.

[v] Jon Meacham, *American Gospel: God, the Founding Fathers, and the Making of a Nation* (New York: Random House, 2006), 41.

[vi] John Fea, *Was America Founded as a Christian Nation?* (Louisville, KY: Westminster John Knox, 2011), 81.

[vii] Ibid., 85.

[viii] William Barlow, *The Sum and Substance of the Hampton Court Conference* (London: Matthew Law, 1604), 83. Note: Sometimes the date for the Hampton Court Conference is given as 1603 or 1603/1604. During the time of the Hampton Court Conference, England was still using the Julian calendar, which recognized March 25 as the first day of the year. Thus, following the Julian calendar, the date would have been 1603. However, in 1752 Great Britain and its colonies switched to the Gregorian calendar. If we are to date the Hampton Court Conference by the Gregorian calendar, the date would be 1604—the date employed in this book.

[ix] *World History* (Pensacola, FL: A Beka Book, 2009), 184.

[x] William Bradford, *History of Plymouth Plantation*, ed. Charles Deane (Boston: n.p., 1856), 24.

NOTES

[xi] William Bradford, 1590–1657, was a passenger on the Mayflower and leader among the Puritans. Bradford wrote a book entitled *History of Plymouth Plantation*, sometimes referred to as *Of Plymouth Plantation*, published in full in 1856. Notably this became America's first history book and earned Bradford the title "Father of American History."

[xii] Paul Johnson, *A History of the American People* (New York: HarperCollins, 1997), 29.

[xiii] Erik Bruun and Jay Crosby, *Our Nation's Archive: The History of the United States in Documents* (New York: Black Dog & Leventhal Publishers, 1999), 43–44. Note: Concerning the Mayflower Compact, the original document has been lost to time, thus several different versions of this document exist.

[xiv] John Fea, *Was America Founded as a Christian Nation?*, 88.

[xv] Francis Newton Thorpe, *The Federal and State Constitutions Colonial Charters, and Other Organic Laws of the States, Territories, and Colonies Nor or Heretofore Forming The United States of America* (Washington, D.C.: Government Printing Office, 1909), 7:3784.

[xvi] The Constitutions of the Several States of the Union and United States, Including the Declaration of Independence and Articles of Confederation (New York: A. S. Barnes & Co., 1853), 245.

[xvii] Francis Newton Thorpe, *The Federal and State Constitutions Colonial Charters, and Other Organic Laws of the States, Territories, and Colonies Nor or Heretofore Forming The United States of America*, 3:1857.

[xviii] Ibid.

[xix] Ibid., 4:2454.

[xx] Ibid.

[xxi] Ibid., 3:1677–1678.

[xxii] Ibid., 3:1689–1690.

[xxiii] Ibid., 1:534.

NOTES

[xxiv]Thomas Williams Bicknell, *The History of the State of Rhode Island and Providence Plantations* (New York: The American Historical Society, 1920), 3:975. On the same page referenced is this comment: "It is true that Roger Williams and others had planted at Providence in 1636, but no formal government was established over that community until 1449, as Mr. Williams did not exercise, if he possessed, the power of organization."

[xxv]Francis Newton Thorpe, *The Federal and State Constitutions Colonial Charters, and Other Organic Laws of the States, Territories, and Colonies Nor or Heretofore Forming The United States of America*, 6:3211–3212.

[xxxvi]Ibid., 1:558.

[xxvii]Ibid., 1:566.

[xxviii]Ibid., 5:2743.

[xxix]Ibid., 5:2793.

[xxx]Ibid., 6:3255–3256.

[xxxi]Ibid., 5:2459.

[xxxii]Ibid., 5:2597–2598.

[xxxiii]Ibid., 5:2636–2637

[xxxiv]Ibid., 5:3036.

[xxxv]Ibid., 5:3082.

[xxxvi]Ibid., 5:3085.

[xxxvii]Ibid., 2:773.

[xxxviii]Ibid., 2:784.

[xxxix]The debate on whether or not slavery is biblical has existed in America for centuries. Yes, the Bible allowed slavery, but with specific limitations. For example, slaves were to be treated humanely (Exodus 21:20, 26, 32) and were not to be stolen (Deuteronomy 24:7). Both of these prohibitions were often disregarded in early America. Most slaves were indeed stolen from Africa, and many were also treated inhumanely.

NOTES

[xl] Jon Meacham, *American Gospel*, 7.

[xli] John Fea, *Was America Founded as a Christian Nation?*, 96.

[xlii] Edmund Cody Burnett, T*he Continental Congress* (Westport, CT: Greenwood Press, 1941), 5.

[xliii] Ibid., 19–20.

[xliv] Ibid., 20.

[xlv] Ibid., 23.

[xlvi] Carpenter's Hall is now known as Independence Hall.

[xlvii] The name "Continental Congress" was not the official designation of the assembly so called. Officially, from its inception in September 1, 1774 to the adoption of the Articles of Confederation (drafted 1777, signed 1778, and ratified 1781) it was simply "The Congress." After the Articles of Confederation it then became "The United States in Congress Assembled." For a time the title "The General Congress" was in vogue. To add to the complexity of this matter, some historians draw distinctions between the Continental Congress and the Congress of the Confederation. And while valid reasons exist for the selection and employment of these strict titles, I have chosen to simply refer to said body as the Continental Congress. After all, there was no essential change in the fundamental character of Congress from 1774 to 1789. Also, "Continental Congress" was the name given to this assembly by the Library of Congress, which has edited the minutes. In addition, this book strives to eliminate tedious discussions and technical terms when possible. The goal is to present an accurate, straightforward, easy-to-understand picture of the relationship between Congress and the Bible.

[xlviii] Worthington Chancey Ford, ed., *Journals of the Continental Congress 1774–1789* (Washington, D.C.: Government Printing Office, 1904), 1:26.

[xlix] Ibid.

[l] Ibid.

[li] Ibid., 27.

NOTES

[liii] Charles Francis Adams, *Familiar Letters of John Adams and His Wife Abigail Adams during the Revolution* (New York: Hurd and Houghton, 1876), 37–8.

[liii] Betty Burnett, The Continental Congress: *A Primary Source History of the Formation of America's New Government* (New York: Rosen, 2004), 21.

[liv] Edmund Cody Burnett, The Continental Congress, 41.

[lv] William Wirt, *Sketches of the Life and Character of Patrick Henry* (Philadelphia: James Webster, 1819), 123.

[lvi] "Religion and the Congress of the Confederation, 1774–89," < http://www.loc.gov/exhibits/religion/rel04.html> (accessed 31 July 2012).

[lvii] "A Declaration by the Representatives of the United Colonies of North-America, Now Met in Congress at Philadelphia, Setting Forth the Causes and Necessity of Their Taking Up Arms," <http://avalon.law.yale.edu/18th_century/arms.asp> (accessed 1 August 2012).

[lviii] "Proclamation of Rebellion," < http://www.britannia.com/history/docs/procreb.html> (accessed 1 August 2012).

[lix] "Religion and the Congress of the Confederation, 1774–89," < http://www.loc.gov/exhibits/religion/rel04.html> (accessed 31 July 2012).

[lx] These proclamations were made on March 29, 1779 and November 28, 1782. Worthington Chancey Ford, Journals of the Continental Congress 1774–1789, 4:425.

[lxii] Larry P. Arnn, *The Founder's Key: The Divine and Natural Connection Between the Declaration and the Constitution and What We Risk by Losing It* (Nashville, TN: Thomas Nelson, 2012), 35–36.

[lxiii] Ibid., 8.

[lxiv] Francis A. Schaeffer, *A Christian Manifesto* (Westchester, IL: Crossway Books, 1981), 103.

NOTES

[lxv] Ibid., 117.

[lxvi] Ibid.

[lxvii] John Fea, *Was America Founded as a Christian Nation?*, 120.

[lxviii] Worthington Chancey Ford, *Journals of the Continental Congress 1774–1789*, 5:517–518.

[lxix] "Religion and the Congress of the Confederation, 1774–89," <http://www.loc.gov/exhibits/religion/rel04.html> (accessed 31 July 2012).

[lxx] Worthington Chancey Ford, *Journals of the Continental Congress 1774–1789*, 5:431.

[lxxi] Edmund Cody Burnett, *The Continental Congress*, 223.

[lxxii] "Articles of Confederation," http://www.archives.gov/exhibits/charters/charters_of_freedom_4.html> (accessed 6 August 2012).

[lxxiii] Ibid.

[lxxiv] "Religion and the Congress of the Confederation, 1774–89," < http://www.loc.gov/exhibits/religion/rel04.html> (accessed 31 July 2012).

[lxxv] "Treaty of Paris," http://memory.loc.gov/cgi-bin/ampage?collId=llsl&fileName=008/llsl008.db&recNum=93 (accessed 6 August 2012).

[lxxvi] Gaillard Hunty, ed., *Journals of the Continental Congress 1774–1789* (Washington, D.C.: Government Printing Office, 1912), 21:1076.

[lxxvii] Larry Arnn, *The Founder's Key*, 84.

[lxxviii] Jon Meacham, *American Gospel*, 89.

[lxxix] Larry Arnn, *The Founder's Key: The Divine and Natural Connection Between the Declaration and the Constitution and What We Risk by Losing It*, 10.

NOTES

[lxxx] Derek H. Davis, *Religion and The Continental Congress 1774–1789* (New York: Oxford University Press, 2000), 65.

[lxxxi] Nathon O. Hatch and Mark A. Noll, eds., *The Bible in America: Essays in Cultural History* (New York: Oxford University Press, 1982), 39.

[lxxxii] Jerry Newcomb, *The Book that Made America: How the Bible Formed our Nation* (Ventura, CA: Nordskog Publishing, 2009), 56.

[lxxxiii] Gilman Marston Ostrander, *The Evolutionary Outlook 1875–1900* (Clio, MI: Marston Press, 1971), 1.

[lxxxiv] Gregg L. Frazer, *The Religious Beliefs of America's Founders: Reason, Revelation, and Revolution* (Lawrence, KS: University Press of Kansas, 2012), 22.

[lxxxv] Ibid., 40.

[lxxxvi] Daniel L. Dreisbach, Mark David Hall, and Jeffry H. Morrison, eds., *The Forgotten Founders on Religion and Public Life* (Notre Dame, IN: University of Notre Dame Press, 2009), 3.

[lxxxvii] Gregg L. Frazer, *The Religious Beliefs of America's Founders*, 18.

[lxxxviii] Ibid.

[lxxxix] Ibid., 71.

[xc] Ibid.

[xci] David L. Holmes, *The Faiths of the Founding Fathers* (New York: Oxford University Press, 2006), 28.

[xcii] Ibid.

[xciii] Edwin S. Gaustad, *Faith of the Founders: Religion and the New Nation 1776–1826* (Waco, TX: Baylor University Press, 2011), 49.

NOTES

[xciv] Ibid., 61.

[xcv] Ibid., 63.

[xcvi] Peter A. Lillback, *George Washington's Sacred Fire* (Bryn Mawr, PA: Providence Forum Press, 2006), 29, 40.

[xcvii] Gregg L. Frazer, *The Religious Beliefs of America's Founders*, 197.

[xcviii] Peter A. Lillback, *George Washington's Sacred Fire*, 41.

[xcix] Gregg L. Frazer, *The Religious Beliefs of America's Founders*, 198, 201.

[c] Ibid., 199.

[ci] Peter A. Lillback, *George Washington's Sacred Fire*, 48.

[cii] Steven Waldman, *Founding Faith* (New York: Random House, 2008), 58.

[ciii] Peter A. Lillback, *George Washington's Sacred Fire*, 26.

[civ] Gregg L. Frazer, *The Religious Beliefs of America's Founders*, 207.

[cv] Ibid., 254.

[cvi] Peter A. Lillback, *George Washington's Sacred Fire*, 43.

[cvii] Ibid., 74–9.

[cviii] Gregg L. Frazer, *The Religious Beliefs of America's Founders*, 200.

[cix] Peter A. Lillback, *George Washington's Sacred Fire*, 312, 314.

[cx] Ibid., 34.

[cxi] Ibid., 323.

[cxii] Ibid.

[cxiii] Ibid., 307.

NOTES

[cxiv] Ibid.

[cxv] The Jefferson Bible (Washington, D.C.: Smithsonian Institution, 2011), 12.

[cxvi] John Fea, *Was America Founded as a Christian Nation?*, 203.

[cxvii] Gregg L. Frazer, *The Religious Beliefs of America's Founders*, 13.

[cxviii] Ibid., 141.

[cxix] Ibid.

[cxx] John Fea, *Was America Founded as a Christian Nation?*, 206.

[cxxi] Ibid., 204.

[cxxii] Gregg L. Frazer, *The Religious Beliefs of America's Founders*, 146.

[cxxiii] Ibid., 154.

[cxxiv] John Fea, *Was America Founded as a Christian Nation?*, 205.

[cxxv] Gregg L. Frazer, *The Religious Beliefs of America's Founders*, 28.

[cxxvi] In July 2012 I visited the Library of Congress (Thomas Jefferson Building) and Thomas Jefferson's Library, an exhibit displaying a reconstruction of Jefferson's library. I counted 57 individual books that could be classified Bibles. This does not necessarily mean 57 Bibles, for some Bibles were issued in more than one volume. Also, these Bibles were in numerous languages.

[cxxvii] Gregg L. Frazer, *The Religious Beliefs of America's Founders*, 136.

[cxxviii] Ibid.

[cxxix] John Fea, *Was America Founded as a Christian Nation?*, 206.

[cxxx] Ibid.

[cxxxi] Ibid., 207.

NOTES

[cxxxii] The Jefferson Bible, 7.

[cxxxiii] Ibid., 11.

[cxxxiv] Ibid., 27.

[cxxxv] Ibid.

[cxxxvi] Ibid., 30.

[cxxxvii] Ibid.

[cxxxviii] Ibid., 34.

[cxxxix] Daniel Dreisbach, *The Forgotten Founders on Religion and Public Life*, 150.

[cxl] Ibid.

[cxli] John Fea, *Was America Founded as a Christian Nation?*, 234.

[cxlii] David L. Holmes, *The Faiths of the Founding Fathers*, 158.

[cxliii] Daniel L. Dreisbach, *The Forgotten Founders on Religion and Public Life*, 151.

[cxliv] Ibid.

[cxlv] Ibid.

[cxlvi] Ibid.

[cxlvii] Ibid.

[cxlviii] John Fea, *Was America Founded as a Christian Nation?*, 235.

[cxlix] Ibid.

[cl] Daniel L. Dreisbach, *The Forgotten Founders on Religion and Public Life*, 165.

[cli] Stephen Northop, ed. *A Cloud of Witnesses* (Reprint, Portland, OR: American Heritage Ministries, 1987), 251.

Notes

[clii] Paul C. Gutjahr, *An American Bible: A History of the Good Book in the United States, 1777–1880* (Standford, CA: Stanford University Press, 1999), 11.

[cliii] "John Jay," <http://www.americanbiblehistory.com/john_jay.html> (accessed 26 October 2012).

[cliv] Dave Miller, "How Important is the Bible to America's Survival?," <http://www.apologeticspress.org/apcontent.aspx?category=7&article=2702> (accessed 21 December 2012).

[clv] Paul C. Gutjahr, *An American Bible*, 95.

[clvi] "John Jay," <http://www.americanbiblehistory.com/john_jay.html> (accessed 26 October 2012).

[clvii] David L. Holmes, *The Faiths of the Founding Fathers*, 160.

[clviii] Ibid.

[clix] Daniel L. Dreisbach, *The Forgotten Founders on Religion and Public Life*, 42.

[clx] David L. Holmes, *The Faiths of the Founding Fathers*, 145.

[clxi] John Fea, *Was America Founded as a Christian Nation?*, 238.

[clxii] Daniel L. Dreisbach, *The Forgotten Founders on Religion and Public Life*, 46.

[clxiii] Ibid.

[clxiv] David L. Holmes, *The Faiths of the Founding Fathers*, 146.

[clxv] Ibid.

[clxvi] Daniel L. Deisbach, *The Forgotten Founders on Religion and Public Life*, 46.

[clxvii] John Fea, *Was America Founded as a Christian Nation?*, 239.

[clxviii] Daniel L. Dreisbach, *The Forgotten Founders on Religion and Public Life*, 49.

[clxix] Ibid.

NOTES

[clxx] John Fea, *Was America Founded as a Christian Nation?*, 242–243.

[clxxi] Ibid., 239.

[clxxii] Daniel L. Dreisbach, *The Forgotten Founders on Religion and Public Life*, 51.

[clxxiii] James H. Hutson, *Religion and the Founding of the American Republic* (Washington, D.C.: Library of Congress, 1998), 56.

[clxxiv] Margaret T. Hills, "An Historical Preface to the American Bible Society Aiken Bible Facsimile" (New York: Arno Press, 1968), preface.

[clxxv] Worthington Chancey Ford, ed., *Journals of the Continental Congress 1774–1789* (Washington, D.C.: Government Printing Office, 1907), 8:733–734.

[clxxvi] Ibid.

[clxxvii] See James H. Hutson, *Religion and the Founding of the American Republic* (Washington, D.C.: Library of Congress, 1998), 56; Derek H. Davis, *Religion and the Continental Congress 1774–1789* (New York: Oxford University Press, 2000), 146; Paul C. Gutjahr, *An American Bible: A History of the Good Book in the United States, 1777–1880* (Stanford, CA: Stanford University Press, 1999), 20.

[clxxviii] Derek H. Davis, *Religion and the Continental Congress 1774–1789*, 146.

[clxxix] Margaret T. Hills, "An Historical Preface to the American Bible Society Aiken Bible Facsimile," preface.

[clxxx] Derek H. Davis, *Religion and the Continental Congress 1774–1789*, 146.

[clxxxi] Margaret T. Hills, "An Historical Preface to the American Bible Society Aiken Bible Facsimile," preface.

[clxxxii] Robert R. Dearden, Jr. and Douglas S. Watson, T*he Bible of the Revolution* (Greenwood, IN: Jonathan Byrd's Rare Books & Bibles, 1995), 14; Paul C. Gutjahr, *An American Bible: A History of the Good Book in the United States, 1777–1880*, 21.

NOTES

[clxxxiii]Derek H. Davis, *Religion and the Continental Congress 1774–1789*, 146; Paul C. Gutjahr, *An American Bible: A History of the Good Book in the United States, 1777–1880*, 21.

[clxxxiv]Margaret T. Hills, "An Historical Preface to the American Bible Society Aiken Bible Facsimile," preface.

[clxxxv]Gaillard Hunt, ed., *Journals of the Continental Congress 1774–1789* (Washington, D.C.: Government Printing Office, 1907), 19:91.

[clxxxvi]Margaret T. Hills, "An Historical Preface to the American Bible Society Aiken Bible Facsimile," preface.

[clxxxvii]Gaillard Hunt, ed., *Journals of the Continental Congress 1774–1789* (Washington, D.C.: Government Printing Office, 1907), 23:572–574.

[clxxxviii]Robert R. Dearden, Jr. and Douglas S. Watson, *The Bible of the Revolution* (Greenwood, IN: Jonathan Byrd's Rare Books & Bibles, 1995), 27–28.

[clxxxix]Ibid.

[cxc]Ibid.

[cxci]Derek H. Davis, *Religion and the Continental Congress 1774–1789*, 146.

[cxcii]Gaillard Hunt, ed., *Journals of the Continental Congress 1774–1789* (Washington, D.C.: Government Printing Office, 1907), 23:572–574.

[cxciii]Derek H. Davis, *Religion and the Continental Congress 1774–1789*, 148.

[cxciv]Richard G. Lee, *In God We Still Trust* (Nashville, TN: Thomas Nelson, 2009), 91.

[cxcv]Ibid., 34.

[cxcvi]Nathon O. Hatch and Mark A. Noll, eds., *The Bible in America: Essays in Cultural History*, 121.

[cxcvii]Ibid.

NOTES

[cxcviii] Ibid., 121–122.

[cxcix] Ibid., 122.

[cc] Ibid.

[cci] "Spiritual Heritage," <http://www.allabouthistory.org/spiritual-heritage> (accessed 5 June 2012).

[ccii] "Proclamation, February 3, 1983," <http://www.reagan.utexas.edu/archives/speeches/1983/20383b> (accessed 21 December 2012).

[cciii] Jerry Newcombe, *The Book that Made America*, 198.

[cciv] Ibid.

[ccv] Ibid.

[ccvi] Ibid.

[ccvii] Stephen Mansfield, *Ten Tortured Words*, (Nashville, TN:Thomas Nelson, 2007), 24.

[ccviii] Ibid.

[ccvix] Ibid.

[ccx] Ibid., 25.

[ccxi] Ibid., 25–26.

[ccxii] Ibid., 62

[ccxiii] Ibid., 39

[ccxiv] Ibid., 45

[ccxv] Ibid., 49-50

[ccxvi] Ibid., 74

[ccxvii] Ibid., 75–76

[ccxviii] David C. Gibbs, *One Nation Under God: Ten Things Every Christian Should Know About the Founding of America* (Seminole, FL: Christian Law Association, 2006), 325.

CPSIA information can be obtained at www.ICGtesting.com
Printed in the USA
BVOW031112280213

314370BV00003BA/9/P